In this controversial and important book two leading educationalists rip away the veils of mythology surrounding British education. They attack the examination system, the fallacy of 'good' schools, and the theory that because Enoch Powell is a professor of Greek he should automatically be respected as an expert on race relations. The whole concept of teachers being 'experts' because they are teachers is explored.

R. E. Bell is a lecturer in Educational Studies at the Open University. He took his first degree in English and archaeology at Cambridge and later studied education and psychology at Trinity College Dublin and Edinburgh University, where he was later a lecturer. He is editor of the journal *Scottish Educational Studies*.

Dr N. D. C. Grant was born in Glasgow and educated at Inverness Royal Academy and Glasgow University where he read English. After two years in the Army, he returned to pursue further studies in education leading to the M.Ed. and Ph.D. degrees. He is now Reader in Educational Studies at the University of Edinburgh.

Robert Bell and
Nigel Grant

A Mythology of British Education

Panther

Granada Publishing Limited
First published in 1974 by Panther Books Ltd
Frogmore, St Albans, Herts AL2 2NF
Copyright © Robert Bell & Nigel Grant 1973
Made and printed in Great Britain by
Richard Clay (The Chaucer Press) Ltd
Bungay, Suffolk
Set in Linotype Plantin

Contents

The mortallest enemy unto knowledge, and that which hath done the greatest execution upon truth, hath been a peremptory adherence unto Authority, and more especially, the establishing of our belief upon the dictates of Antiquity.

(Sir Thomas Browne, 1672)

It is perfectly true that an experienced anthropologist, visiting a 'new' primitive society for the first time and working with the aid of competent interpreters, may be able, after a stay of only a few days, to develop in his own mind a fairly comprehensive 'model' of how the social system works, but it is also true that if he stays for six months and learns to speak the language very little of that original 'model' will remain. Indeed the task of understanding how the system works will by then appear even more formidable than it did just two days after his first arrival ... To anthropologists who have had a wider and more varied range of field experience, it seems all too obvious that this initial model is little more than an amalgam of the observer's own prejudiced presuppositions.

(Edmund Leach, *Lévi-Strauss*, Fontana, 1970, p. 19)

CHAPTER ONE

THE FOLKLORE OF EDUCATION

The trouble with myth is not that it is wrong, but that it is irrational and believed. Wrong statements can be refuted by evidence, faulty deductions can be subjected to the litmus test of logic. But myth is exempt from all this. One does not have to prove anything, simply state what is 'known'. There is no need to bother with logical inconsistencies, any more than the Greeks were bothered about placing the gods in heaven *and* on an identifiable mountain, for myth imposes a logic of its own. Above all, it has the power not only to explain how things are, but to give them an apparent justification. Demonstration of fact or value thus becomes unnecessary; assertion, if it carries enough authority, will do.

Myth-making is not confined to the ancient world, nor has it anything to do with 'the childhood of the intellect'. The conventional wisdom of the Victorians took it for granted that myth, like fairy-stories, was the mode of thought of a more primitive age, left behind by the advancing tide of reason and progress. Some of them liked to date the breakthrough from Newton:

> Nature and nature's way lay hid in night;
> God said, 'Let Newton be!' and all was light.

We are not so sure about the inevitability of progress now – the notion of modern man as an increasingly rational being has taken a bad beating this century – but we are still inclined to consign myth to some pre-rational stage that we like to think we have outgrown.

But surely this is too simple. Myth and rationality have co-existed since ancient times. The Babylonian priests made telling advances in mathematics and astronomy, and at the same time tried to read the future from the bumps on the liver of a sheep. Nor are the giants of the enlightenment exempt: Newton, for all his seminal contributions to the sciences that made possible a

rational account of the universe, spent much of his time comb-
ing the Book of Daniel for hidden prophecies, and regarded this
as his life's work. Kepler (if Koestler is right) made his discoveries on the working of the solar system not in spite of his
obsession with the five perfect solids, but because of it.[1] Sophis-
tication and belief in myth have never made strange bedfellows.
To take a particularly nasty example, clumsy and vicious forg-
eries such as the *Protocols of the Elders of Zion* were accepted
not only by obsessional neurotics like the last Russian empress or
half-educated fanatics like Rosenberg or Hitler, but by not a few
cultivated men. One of them, Paul de Lagarde, was a university
professor and an orientalist of distinction who, though well-
equipped to see through the myth in five minutes, played a
major part in disseminating it.[2] Race and politics, admittedly,
are subjects notoriously resistant to rational analysis, but there is
an abundant growth of lower-key mythology around practically
every social question of our time.

Take the case of the Swedish suicides, a popular tale with the
late President Eisenhower and a host of others. Stated crudely
(and it usually is) it goes like this: Sweden has a high living
standard and the most advanced cradle-to-grave welfare and
medical service in the world; yet, in this paragon of a welfare
state, people kill themselves more readily than anywhere else.
Clearly, socialised medicine and soft living have rotted their
moral fibre, providing thereby a warning for us all. One can object that the *recording* of suicides is affected by legal and religious considerations, and that even if the facts were as stated the
deductions are, to say the least, arguable; one can even point out
that in fact Sweden does not have the highest suicide rate. But
such objections have little effect. Eisenhower could have
checked the facts if he had wished, but did not; he was dealing
in myth, where fact is what is believed when emotionally necessary to support a point of view. This particular myth has been
exploded often enough, but refuses to die; like so many others,
it has proved too useful.[3]

Turning from the present to the past, consider the popularity
of the Decline and Fall of the Roman Empire[4] among critics of
what they term our 'permissive society'. According to this particular body of myth, the Roman Empire 'fell' because of the
sexual preoccupations of its citizens, thus providing our own

society with warnings of terrible things which will follow from the pill, mini-skirts, see-through blouses and nude films. Useful though all this may be as a rhetorical trope, it will hardly do as a serious analysis. There are too many imponderables, too many uncontrolled variables. The decline of the Roman Empire was a complex phenomenon and stretched over several centuries – not a bad run for a morally decadent civilisation. The sexual proclivities of its leading personalities are, at best, sketchily documented from gossip-column material, but as far as these go they suggest that picturesque activities were in full swing even before the Empire was properly established. The more enterprising emperors in this line are as likely to turn up among the early Julio-Claudians (notably Tiberius) as among the later wearers of the purple. It is difficult to connect the undoubted, if slow, political decline with what little is known of contemporary sex-life. Interestingly, adherents of this singular interpretation of history rarely explain what was so wonderful about the Roman Empire anyway; if we can wrest morality away from sex for the moment, there is ample evidence that political thuggery and administrative corruption were standard practice of a successful Rome from the days of the Republic onwards, until the Empire eventually fizzled out into ghostly legal fictions. Nor is it explained why the final collapse should be thought startling enough to require a hunt for sexual causes; given the crudity of its organisation, it might rather be wondered why this particular empire lasted so much longer than any of its successors. But this is not really the point. We are not dealing with a serious historical debate, but the plaything of prurient moralists looking for an argument. It has the weight of apparent erudition and satisfies emotional rather than rational needs. In such cases, proof is unnecessary; assertion is all.

Myth of this kind flourishes with special luxuriance in those areas of human concern where many are vitally affected but few are well informed. There is not a great deal of myth in biology, astronomy or palaeontology. True, some popular fiction shows dinosaurs as contemporaries of mammoths and men, or uses light-years as a measure of time, but this is simple ignorance, not myth; no emotional case depends on its being taken seriously. Equally, it is unlikely that there is much mechanical myth, for the rather different reason that misconceptions are all too easily exploded when things fail to work. However, in many areas of general concern in which no esoteric language is needed, myth still flourishes. There are countless myths that survive elementary factual exposure in politics, race relations, and in medicine (especially where sex, pregnancy, cancer or slimming are involved). It is, for example, widely asserted that class-solidarity in voting is particularly characteristic of the British working class; if this were true, there would have been constant Labour government since the late 1920s (see J. Blondel, *Voters, Parties and Leaders*, 1968). It is still widely believed that masturbation is and sexual intercourse can be physically and mentally debilitating (see Alex Comfort, *The Anxiety Makers*, 1969), that Orientals have slanting eyes (see an Oriental) or that coloured immigrants flood the labour market, yet manage at the same time to live entirely on social security (no comment). Such firm beliefs survive not because they are true (they are not) but because they are emotionally satisfying aids to contentions which are difficult or even impossible to justify on coldly rational grounds.

Education is supposed to be concerned with reason and intelligence, to be run by people of considerable mental ability, and so forth. But it lends itself in practice to at least as much superstition and myth as any other human activity. Most people are involved in some way with education; much of their own or their children's personal and social status seems to depend upon it, and they are naturally less likely to regard education as a remote specialism. At the same time, educational discourse is all too often imprecise, leaving ample room for the woolly generalisation or the untested assertion. Few people would claim medical omniscience on the strength of having had an injection or two and a minor operation, few claim legal expertise after drawing up a will or being fined for speeding, but we have all been to school and hence know all about teachers and their concerns. (Not quite all perhaps; school teaching still carries some social status, and large sections of the public are prepared to concede to professors of anything from Sanskrit to seismology a degree of expertise on almost any matter, educational or other, which is quite astonishing to anyone who takes a closer look. With equal recklessness they deny that students can have valid views on anything, and insist that their work must be a 24-hour-a-day process quite incompatible with political or any other activity except perhaps having regular haircuts.) As we shall see later, all sorts of insecurities, snobberies, vested interests and beliefs about the nature of oneself and society depend on being able to believe something about education, rational or not. Nor is this only a lay phenomenon; many teachers and academics, for instance, are if anything more prone to accept and retail educational superstitions than the public at large. Arguably, they are by virtue of their education more knowledgeable and critical than most; but they are also more directly involved, and their own security all too often requires them to keep their critical faculties for special occasions rather than turn them upon themselves.

It may be that education does not readily lend itself to myths as wild as that of the *Protocols of the Elders of Zion*, but the educational equivalents of the suicidal Swedes and the sex-mad Romans crop up again and again. We heard much of the 'antiquity' of the public and grammar schools, of the 'traditional' boarding school ethos, or the ancient role of the universities as guardians of disinterested scholarship and academic freedom stretching back to the Middle Ages. Thus, the emotional weight of tradition is pressed into service, and tradition counts for much in British society still, at least among those who make the decisions. Whether we are being invited to rejoice in the present state of affairs (God's in his heaven, all's right with the world) or to bewail the passing of a Golden Age, the assumption of accumulated wisdom is allowed to pre-empt more straightforward argument. Similarly, we may be offered tales, not of the past, but of other lands. It has often been asserted with confidence that, whatever our own failings may be, at least our children are more broadly educated than the Russians with their diet of mathematics and Marxism, and much better educated than the Americans, who flock into raw and inexperienced universities for M.A.s in make-up and doctorates in car-driving. (In the Jeremiah-type versions, these are Horrible Warnings of 'the way we are going'.) It is 'known' that examinations test ability and predict performance; clever children will 'find their own level' (or, alternatively, will be 'held back' if taught in unstreamed classes or even unselective schools). Games are good for 'character', Latin for logic, mathematics for accuracy and higher education in almost anything for generalised wisdom. We hear talk of 'good' schools, and it is assumed that we all know (and agree) what 'good' means. As for 'discipline', 'standards' and the like, there may be argument about the best way to achieve them, but no one in his senses would deny that they exist or are easily recognised. The list could be prolonged indefinitely.

These mythological phenomena constitute a mixed bag, to say the least. Some involve the retailing of simple untruth, as we shall see, some involve at best half-truths posing as facts, some are meaningless, and some come into the category of statements that escape close examination by asserting the unverifiable or the unquantifiable. 'Clever children will find their own level' is a classic example of the last: obviously, children who do not come out 'on top' are assumed on this view not to be clever at all, and it is pretty safe to go on asserting it, logically suspect though it is. But all these assertions do have this much in common: they are stated, not argued, believed, not demonstrated, and their job is to shore up a case, not to illuminate one. They are the educational equivalents of the beliefs that thunder curdles milk, that spilling salt brings bad luck, that Africans have extra thick skulls or, for that matter, that Sweden has the highest suicide rate or that the Roman Empire collapsed from sexual over-indulgence. It is high time they were required to present their credentials for closer examination.

Myth is not, of course, all of a piece, nor is credulity evenly spread. Just as there were Greeks who took the tales of Kronos swallowing his children quite literally, so are there many today who accept the grosser educational superstitions without demur. (Call them the lay public if you will; it includes some teachers and many professors, since everyone is a layman with respect to most subjects, a point which current educational myth does much to obscure.) Those who are most directly involved in the process might be expected to know better, but often act as disseminators of myth if their own standing depends on it. Intelligence, after all, is no guarantee against stupidity. An hour or two watching the knife-fighting on a university Senate or Council soon disposes of the notion that academics are necessarily detached, critical or civilised when vital interests are involved; more articulate they may be, but it is soon obvious that

scientists are no more sceptical or philosophers more philosophical than anyone else. Yet the notion of *general* academic
competence persists. The views of Mr Enoch Powell, for example, are open to debate, reasonably enough; what is surprising is the number of people prepared to regard them as rational,
or even indisputable, because he was once a professor of Greek –
an excellent reason for listening with respect to his views on
deponent verbs or choric odes, but hardly giving him a special
claim to be taken seriously on race relations or economics. In
fairness, Mr Powell makes no such claims, but they are made for
him nonetheless. Some are not so scrupulous. Dr Ernest Clax-
ton, Assistant Secretary of the B.M.A., once told a Moral Re-
Armament meeting in London : 'As a doctor I can tell you that
extra- and pre-marital intercourse is medically dangerous, morally degrading and nationally destructive.'[5] It is a point of view,
and of course he is perfectly entitled to argue his case; significantly, however, he did not attempt to do so, but was content to
pronounce on moral matters 'as a doctor', as if his profession
somehow made him an unchallengeable expert. (Perhaps because
he was addressing a lay audience, he did not make it clear how
he managed to distinguish *medically* between pre-marital sex
and the presumably harmless marital variety.) Recently, the
Senate of a Scottish university refused, unlike many others, to
admit any students to membership on the grounds that they
were not competent to judge academic matters. In the same
university, professors of microbiology or economics are frequently called upon to judge the suitability of curricula in, say,
Arabic or animal husbandry; why they are thought more capable of this than graduate students who have actually taken
such courses is not altogether clear. The high degree of specialist competence that put them (one assumes) in their chairs is
somehow taken to imply an overall competence. It seems that
the general public is prepared to concede this as a rule; note, for
instance, the eagerness of many political lobbies to strengthen
their case, however worthy, by putting a few professors (bishops
and actresses too, if possible) among the signatories of their
appeals. The contributors to the Black Papers in education included many academics, some of them of considerable distinction in their own fields; the fact that very few of them were
educationists and that hardly any had professional experience of

primary or secondary education did not prevent these publications from being taken seriously in many educational and political circles and by many sections of the public.

Just as there are many varieties of myth-maker and myth-believer, there are different levels of myth, ranging from disconnected minor superstitions of the black-cat-crossing-the-road type to highly-organised cosmologies like those of the ancient world. Like classical myth, too, they vary in the extent to which they rely on pure fiction and how much, like the Homeric poems, they weave strands of fact into the fabric.

First, there are myths based on assertions that are simply and demonstrably wrong, such as 'the grammar schools have always been free of state control' or 'the Russians now have one of the most highly selective systems in the world'. These can be relatively easily dealt with though, on previous showing, it will take more than that to put them out of circulation. Rather more common are those which have some element of truth in them, just enough to suggest that we are in the realm of fact, but not enough to bear the weight of the interpretation placed on them. Many of the assertions about educational tradition come into this class. To take rather a trivial example, there is a school in Edinburgh, selective and fee-paying, whose late headmaster was much given to descanting on the antiquity of its traditions and arguing from that against 'tampering' with it (*i.e.* trying to absorb it into the national system). He would point with pride to the building which, indeed, dates back to the beginning of the seventeenth century. What he did not mention was that it was an orphanage and primary school for most of its history, becoming a secondary school only in 1885. Similarly, a secondary school in the Scottish Highlands claims an unbroken history of over seven centuries, and announces this in a bold Latin hexameter over the entrance: 'Septingenti annos sum Boreae ego lampas' (For seven hundred years I have been the light of the North). It is perfectly true that there has been a school of some kind in the town for all that time (there has been in most towns), though how far it has enjoyed real continuity is more doubtful. It was certainly not the same kind of institution throughout. If it matters, the school's charter dates from the nineteenth century, the building from the twentieth, and the hexameter from 1953. In the case of both these schools there is some fact at least, but the way in which it is filled out with fiction is mythical, rather like the poet's introduction of the gods as serving combatants in the undoubtedly historical Trojan War.

Then there are the hidden value-judgements in which so much educational discussion is couched. A particular school may be called a 'good' school, a particular type of course is said to provide a 'good' education, a particular practice is claimed to instil 'character', 'leadership', discipline' and so forth. Rarely is there any attempt to define what 'good' (etc.) means, and discussion is likely to revolve around the relative 'goodness' of, say, grammar or comprehensive schools on the terms of the original assertion. Discussion on this level, without examining the implicit values or their relationship to social need, is rather like playing not so much with loaded dice as unmarked dice, like those used by Big Julie in *Guys and Dolls*: 'I had the spots taken off for luck. But I have a good memory; I remember where the spots formerly were.'

Another type of superstition arises from what might be called logical sleight-of-hand. Take for instance the frequent assertion that middle-class parents are those most concerned or informed about education, or even, hilariously enough in a post-Arnoldian and post-Dickensian age, that the middle class is 'cultured' (while the working-class parents, indifferent to the whole business of education, 'prefer to spend their money on what, since the state is not providing it, they would otherwise have to do without, such as cars and drinks and smoking and hair-dos and betting and bingo and so on'.)[6] The value of such statements is obvious enough: they give to what might otherwise look like special pleading for class privilege a gloss of respectable responsibility. But it is a shaky proposition at best. It is probably true that most people who are informed about 'education' (or 'culture', though this is equally hard to define) do belong to the middle classes. Given the connection between personal education and occupation and social class, this is not altogether surprising. But to argue that this applies to the whole class, or anything like it, is absurd; knowing about advantageous schools to get one's children into is hardly the same as awareness of real educational issues. There are, of course, many sections of the middle class whose ignorance of educational matters is quite as impressive as that of their manual counterparts. What we have here is not a sociological statement, but a variant of the 'coals-in-the-bath' myth. It will take some shifting; being able to seem responsible and even disinterested instead of having a keen eye to the main chance is far too valuable a posture to relinquish without a struggle.

Then there is pseudo-scientific myth, the magical quality of processes described in sufficiently arcane terms. Mental testing and examination techniques evoke a superstitious awe more reminiscent of astrology or alchemy than the more critical evaluation appropriate to a scientific technique. This is not to say that such techniques are useless, but that they are often pressed into service in a quite uncritical way. Generally, this is a failing of the layman rather than the specialist; those actually involved in testing are usually well aware of the difficulties and limitations, and with a few odd exceptions (like Professor Lynn in *Black Paper Two*)[7] do not make exaggerated claims for them. How reliable the methods are, how they should be devised, and what use should be made of them are all, quite properly, still matters of scientific controversy.

Even the most precise methods have margins of error, as any psychometrician would be the first to point out. But they are frequently used not as hypotheses or even as useful tools within limits, but as exact and infallible oracular pronouncements. Many teachers and probably most parents, therefore, are quite prepared to accept the results of a ten-minute whittled-down Terman-Merrill on ten-year-olds as the verdict of science. We know of one highly respected, élitist, traditionally 'good' school where over 300 children, mainly of professional parents, are winnowed in this way at the age of *four* to find an intake of fifty; future performance could be predicted about as accurately by closing one's eyes and sticking a pin in the list, but then that would hardly pass as scientific.

Not all the appeals to the spuriously precise are as daft as this, but the collector can find some gems at the other end of the process. Final examinations for honours degrees, especially in non-numerical disciplines, are bound to involve a large element of approximation. One examiner's beta plus is another's alpha minus, one's pass-mark another's fail; the discrepancies can be even wider than this. Of course, the examiners try hard to be fair, and often go to great lengths of cross-checking and discussion of individual cases, but there is bound to be some imprecision (and, often, value-judgements) in the final assessment. This is known to the examiners and realised by most candidates, but is concealed by the necessity under the regulations in most universities to classify passes as first, upper seconds, lower seconds and thirds; in some examinations they even have to be expressed as a percentage. Doubtless some results do fall unambiguously into one category or another, but borderline cases are common. Since employers and many others outside the universities are rarely aware of this, they can hardly be blamed for taking the figures on the graduation scrolls not as approximations but as something clear-cut; but any university teacher should know better than this, having done this job himself. The spectacle, therefore, of committees of professors deciding admissions to higher degree work on the basis of just such marks has an air of comedy about it. It is not as if they feel that they must draw the line somewhere – this would be understandable enough; but a great many of them are convinced that the difference between a 2·1 and a 2·2 is firm, distinct and meaningful. The irony is that such investigations as have been carried out do little to confirm the accuracy of examinations.[8] Astonishingly (when one considers how much any selective procedure is bound to act to some extent as a self-fulfilling prophecy) it turns out that performance in 'A' levels is rather a poor predictor of performance in degree examinations. This has been suspected for years, yet the universities go on being influenced by fine gradations of examination pass with a degree of precision quite useless for predictive purposes. And so on; the desire for accuracy seems to give numbers a magical rather than a scientific appeal.

Finally, we have the supreme illogicality, the simultaneous entertaining of mutually contradictory elements, so characteristic of mythological thinking. One often hears Government spokesmen, for instance, declaring in favour of comprehensive schooling *and* the retention of selective grammar schools. (Even the late Iain Macleod stated that the two types could 'flourish together' – *Times Educational Supplement,* January 1966.)[9] It must be obvious that if comprehensive schools have to coexist to any great extent, they cannot *be* comprehensive; whatever they are called, they can hardly be more than 'secondary modern' schools under another, and possibly less unattractive, title. Tempting though it is, we cannot examine the case for or against comprehensive schooling here, but this is not the point. Declarations in favour of both types simply duck the issue, rather than try to present a case either way; they have the common virtue of mythological thinking in making it seem possible to have one's cake and eat it.

Clearly, myth does not flourish without reason. Classical myth, for instance, long outlived any literal belief due to its convenience as a framework, as conceptual shorthand, as an emotional comforter or as embellishment in literature. Homer made excellent use of it (though his account makes it hard to believe that he took it very seriously), and so do moderns like Graves. Educational myth is not picturesque or dramatic enough for that; its continued currency must be due to some emotional need to believe it, and of course we do not have to look far to find needs in plenty. There is sheer sentimentality; graduates may, for instance, like to think that their mediaeval hoods and gowns link them with the ages, thus assuring them a place in a grand continuity of scholarship. That the universities were quite different institutions (from which few bothered to graduate) until the late nineteenth century, and that even in the ancient universities many of the trappings are modern inventions, is neither here nor there. It is as harmless, and as pointless, as the druidic costumes and rituals at the Eisteddfod (invented by an eighteenth-century Methodist preacher) or the latinised rituals and responses invented at Stowe school during the 1920s.[10] More seriously, though, myth can be a potent booster of prestige for a particular school or university or, by extension, a whole category, which rubs off on those who have been through it. The mere antiquity, real or imagined, of an establishment helps, as does the idea that it is socially select, academically outstanding or both. Anyone who has been to a particular establishment, therefore, even if (or particularly if) he is undistinguished or dim personally, has an interest in seeing that its repute is sustained by whatever means are available. There are countless examples of this, and we shall see later how shaky some of the claims are. Meanwhile, it might be helpful to note the carefully-fostered *esprit de corps* among former pupils (so significantly called 'Old Boys') of some minor public schools. The Old Boys' Club of one such school recently exposed itself on television with a frankness that suggests insensitivity more than anything else. Perhaps the most revealing thing was that against the beery euphoria of the rugger-players and the self-laudatory reunions, those who had achieved any particular distinction were notably absent (not that it would have proved much in any case had they been there). The frantic ritualisation of the institution was, apparently, for those who needed it. This sort of thing suits the institution too, of course; 'Old Boys' can be a useful source of money.

Vested interests may often be served in this way that are difficult to justify on non-mythical lines. Games as a 'character-building' institution (an ill-defined concept in any case) owes much of its continued acceptance to the schools' interest in acquiring prestige through winning games. The connection in its day between 'drill' and 'discipline' had far less to do with any thought-out idea of what discipline was supposed to be than with the availability of a supply of ex-service instructors and a sudden incursion of the military spirit into the schools after the Crimean War. Or consider the claims advanced for the study of the classical languages. There is, of course, a perfectly good case to be made on grounds of interest, but this is not strong enough to attract sufficient numbers; anyway, it is not the one usually offered. What we get instead is vague rhetoric about their unique value in 'training the mind'. There have even been attempts to argue that they have some special contribution to make to moral education through the study of the lives of noble Romans and Greeks, though to make sense this would have to be extraordinarily selective. At times, such special pleading rises to sublime heights of dottiness, as when Sir Compton Mackenzie claimed in *Greece in my Life*, apparently in all seriousness, that allowing pupils to take Russian or German instead would turn us all into Communists. More commonly though, we are told that it is necessary to introduce pupils to the treasure-house of Greco-Roman culture on which so much of our civilisation rests, or that Latin, with its uniquely logical structure, provides an excellent training for logical thinking generally. In the first case, there is a serious point, but it is an odd argument for requiring 'O' level Latin for admission to certain university courses; this is hardly enough to enable one to pick a painful way even through easier authors such as Caesar or Livy, let alone Vergil or Catullus. Homer and the Greek tragedians, of course, remain as remote as ever. If one took the cultural argument seriously, there would be a strong case for starting with Greek right away, rather than Latin with its largely derivative literature. Come to that, the introduction to the treasure-house would surely be better effected by using good translations – but of course that would not call for the lengthy 'mental exercise' of grammatical slog, or provide sufficient jobs. As for the 'logical training' argument, this is hard to defend either linguistically or psychologically. Latin is not a logical language; like any other, it has rules which are no more than generalisations about what actually happens, and they are hedged about by exceptions, usually quite arbitrary. It is grammatically complex, of course, but any benefit that might be gained from wrestling with that could just as well be gained from studying Sanskrit, Serbo-Croat or Lithuanian, which are rather more complex. As for the idea of transfer of ability to general from particular performance, few psychologists have taken this seriously for half a century, except where closely related skills are involved.

Much current mythology is class-based political rationalisation, perhaps at present the commonest type of all. The putative antiquity of certain kinds of schools, and the alleged disinterested concern of the middle class, come neatly into this category, for obvious reasons. So do the strange pleas for the retention of selective schools as separate entities within a comprehensive system. So do the 'more means worse' Jeremiads of the Black Paper tigers. So does much of the present condemnation of attempts to change the structure of the school system as an attack on the traditional freedom and independence of, say, the grammar schools. We shall look more closely later at the uses of words like 'freedom' (oddly selective, as a rule). Meanwhile, it is worth reminding ourselves that whatever may be said about state intervention in the grammar schools, there is nothing whatever new about it. Queen Elizabeth's Council made this abundantly clear in 1580 :

For as much as a great deal of the corruption of religion grown throughout the realm, proceedeth of lewd school masters ... it is thought meet for redress therof, that you cause all such school masters as have charge of children, to be by the Bishop of the diocese ... examined touching their religion: and if they be found corrupt and unworthy, to be displaced ... and fit and sound persons placed in their rooms.[11]

Even the Latin grammar textbook was centrally prescribed. Needless to say, the whole principle of state intervention, quite apart from the merits of any particular invention, is open to discussion; but rational discussion is hindered, not helped, by insisting on the myth of a golden age of freedom from which we are declining fast into totalitarianism. In this, as in so much else, the function of myth is not only to explain and justify the way things are, but to keep them that way.

As the types and functions of myth vary, so do the methods of putting them across. Argument (see any Hansard account of a debate on education) is swathed and often hidden in clouds of rhetoric and mystical language that has more in common with incantation than analysis. The language of much current discussion bears a similar relation to ritual as do the assertions to primitive myth. Incantation, ritual response, sermon, benediction – in one form or another, they are all there. Reiteration, as befits non-rational language, is much in evidence. In a recent letter to *The Times*, Dr A. L. Rowse gave his views on university expansion 'as one qualified to speak', and at the same time provided a fine example of the reiteration technique:

I have spent all my life in a university ... The simple truth is (that) the number of people who effectively profit from a university education, or who are up to it, *is* very limited ... Those of us who have been in the know all our lives know that (the idea that an infinite pool of talent exists) is simply not true. That university expansion has already gone too far, and far too fast, is witnessed by the behaviour of a large minority of students. They are a minority, but anyone with any sense can see that *they should not be there*. They are ruining things for the others ...

Today every chance is given to these students, everything is done for them. I have not expressed my opinion on this matter before, but it is based on long experience and intimate knowledge. The behaviour of this large minority of students is rude, boorish, selfish, inconsiderate, and – quite apart from the time they waste, the equipment they disfigure and destroy – utterly disgraceful.

All people of sense know that they should simply not be at the universities, wasting their and our time.[12]

Quite apart from the absence of a single hard fact or piece of evidence, this passage is a good instance of the common assumption that anything said three times becomes true.

Flowery language is a natural favourite, uplifting and at the same time usefully vague. Examples abound, but a collector's piece can be found in the Fleming Report on the public schools.

A true picture of the Public Schools would have to include a reference to the annual Latin play at Westminster, performed today as laid down in the Statutes of 1560, and also to such an undertaking as the performance of Mr Bernard Shaw's *St Joan* by the boys of one of the older schools to audiences in Strasbourg, Nancy and Paris in the spring of 1939. It would pay attention as much to the educational experiments in work on the land carried out at a very recent foundation, such as Bryanston, as to the rules of Fives at Eton, where the Court in which the game is played is a faithful representation of the space between the buttresses of the fifteenth century Chapel. It would have to take account of the Greek iambics written in Sixth Book at Winchester as well as the work of the metal shops at Oundle, without forgetting the Science taught at the one school or the Classics at the other, and it would have to consider the buildings of the Public Schools from the Chapels of the founders at Winchester or Eton to those of more recent years at Giggleswick, Lancing and Stowe, and to the War Memorial Chapel at Charterhouse completed sixteen years ago. At least the Public Schools have made of themselves real communities, and there may be seen in the education they offer a definite sense of purpose.[13]

We shall have occasion to look more closely at this and other specimens later on. Argument may be in short supply on many issues, but finely-turned rhetoric is plentiful.

As a special side-line, Biblical or Shakespearean imagery, heavy with the wisdom of the ages, is pressed into service. Choice examples are Tibor Szamuely's reference[14] to the 'Gadarene rush' of supporters of comprehensive schooling ('frantic hordes' is not, as far as we know, Biblical), or the case presented in the Hadow Report of 1926 for transferring children from primary to secondary school at the age of eleven:

There is a tide which begins to rise in the veins of youth at the age of eleven or twelve. It is called by the name of adolescence. If that tide can be taken at the flood, and a new voyage begun in the strength and along the flow of its current, we think that it will 'move

on to fortune'. We therefore propose that all children should be
transferred at the age of eleven or twelve . . .[15]

Anyone interested in checking the original will find it in *Julius
Caesar* V, iii – 'There is a tide in the affairs of men which, taken
at the flood, leads on to fortune.' Brutus is using the trope to
persuade Cassius that they should attack immediately; Cassius,
who has offered practical military arguments against this course,
allows himself to be swayed. For what it is worth, Brutus is
proved disastrously wrong by events; but of course it is the tone
that counts, not the meaning. More to the point, the civil servants who drew up the report and seemed so impressed by the
rhetoric probably put their own children in preparatory schools
where the age of transfer is thirteen.

There is also pseudo-scientific language, with statistics
pressed into the hole of cabbalistic signs. Quotes from the great
are popular, almost like readings from the sacred texts; they give
added authority, which is also very useful. The package-deal is
extensively used; bracket a real with a mythical statement, a
reasonable with an unreasonable proposition, and there is a good
chance that the lack of a logical connection will not be noticed.
Some of the Black Paper authors, for example, link legitimate
criticism of some of the work being done in some colleges of
education with modern developments in general and progressive
primary teaching methods in particular, as if they were all part
of the same phenomenon. One of them, Sir Cyril Burt, seeks to
link such methods with the very real (but as far as is known
unconnected) problem of delinquency :

Parents and members of the public at large are beginning to wonder whether the free discipline, or lack of discipline, in the new
permissive school may not be largely responsible for much of the
subsequent delinquency, violence and general unrest that characterise
our permissive society.[16]

No connection is, of course, demonstrated; a few sweeping
statements, the slipping in of 'permissive' at two points, the
question-begging use of 'subsequent', and the thing is done –
without being examined or even described, progressive teaching has been found guilty by association.

There is even (to extend the earlier analogy) a body of noncanonical devotional literature. School-stories, for instance, from *Tom Brown's Schooldays* to *Red Circle School*, help to nourish and spread the assumptions and values of Smith of the Lower Third and Stalky and Co. (Most would gag now on such terrible prigs as *Eric* or John Verney in *The Hill*, but in their heyday these were staple fare for many of those now running and legislating for the educational system of this country.) One has only to contemplate the spectacle of heads of day schools (even in Scotland, normally so conscious of a separate tradition) elaborately constructing prefect systems, games captaincies and 'Houses' which have no relation to any building or corporate body but to which pupils are expected to show loyalty, to reflect that nature sometimes contrives to imitate art.

How much does all this matter? It could be argued that many of these delusions are harmless enough. So they are, in themselves. It does not really matter whether Arnold approved of boarding schools or not, or whether a particular school can trace its origins to the late sixteenth or early twentieth century. The harm is in the approach. In a very real sense, no error is harmless if it distorts the picture, confuses the issue, and puts irrational obstacles in the way of rational discussion. At a time when it is clearer than ever that in education what we do now will affect our children, their children and to a considerable extent the kind of society they will live in, we have to try to be clear about what we are doing. We are not concerned here with contesting or advocating particular policies or values, important though that is; there is room for that elsewhere. But it does seem that if logical discussion is to proceed usefully, there is a need to clear away at least some of the emotional entanglements of myth which so inhibit freedom of action in British education.

REFERENCES

1. Arthur Koestler, *The Sleepwalkers* (Penguin, 1964), pp. 227 ff.
2. Norman Cohn, *Warrant for Genocide* (Penguin, 1970), pp. 188–93.
3. Eisenhower's comments are mentioned in Erwin Stengel, *Suicide and Attempted Suicide* (Penguin), and the implications of religious and legal factors are discussed in Herbert Hendin, *Suicide and Scandinavia*; actual figures from the *Statistical Abstract of Sweden* give Sweden a fairly high rate, but one which lags well

behind a number of other countries, including Hungary, Austria, Finland, Japan, Czechoslovakia, Switzerland and both Germanies. For a general discussion, see Colin Simpson, *The Viking Circle* (Hodder and Stoughton, 1967), pp. 48–52.

4. See for example reference in Hugh Trevor-Roper, *The Rise of Christian Europe* (Thames and Hudson, 1965), p. 26.

5. Quoted by Alex Comfort, *The Anxiety Makers* (Panther, 1968), p. 162.

6. John Highet, *A School of One's Choice* (Blackie, 1969), pp. 268–9.

7. Professor Richard Lynn, in C. B. Cox and A. E. Dyson (Eds.) *Black Paper Two: Crisis in Education.* (Critical Quarterly Society, 1969).

8. *E.g.*, J. Drever, *Godfrey Thompson Lecture*, Edinburgh, 1965.

9. Quoted in Robin Davis, *The Grammar School* (Penguin, 1967), p. 106.

10. 'The school motto was "Sto, persto, praesto" (I stand, I endure, I excel), and at roll-calls (called "stances") in the great circular marble hall ... (we would) answer not "here" or "present" but (I find myself blushing to write it) "Sto" '. Gavin Maxwell, *The House of Elrig* (Pan, 1968), pp. 144–5.

11. T. L. Jarman, *Landmarks in the History of Education* (Murray, 1963), p. 163.

12. Letter in *The Times*, 19 May 1970.

13. *The Public Schools and the General Educational System* (The Fleming Report) (H.M.S.O., 1944), p. 44.

14. In Cox and Dyson, *op. cit.*

15. *The Education of the Adolescent* (The Hadow Report). (H.M.S.O., 1926).

16. In Cox and Dyson, *op. cit.*

CHAPTER TWO

RITUAL AND RHETORIC

Perhaps the greatest enemy of clear thinking about education in Britain today is the dominating use of unexamined words. All too often, attitudes are taken up and decisions made, not because of facts or even of needs but on the basis of assumptions that certain words have a precise and generally recognised usage, or that certain practices and value-systems need not be questioned at all. Fortunately, educational philosophers, R. S. Peters in particular, have become more and more vocal in their demand that such assertions and assumptions should be re-examined, but as yet their pleas have affected only a tiny minority of parents and teachers. While their works figure more and more prominently in the college or university syllabus, any caution developed in such classes seems all too soon forgotten once the students have left the institution if, indeed, they have not already been eroded by the preachings of the philosopher's colleagues, whose own teachings, however scholarly or scientific, are all too often pitted with value-judgements and unexamined assumptions.

For example, how often does one hear not only older politicians and academics but even teachers in their twenties and thirties deploring the coming of comprehensive secondary education on the grounds that it will mean the destruction of 'good' schools? Clearly, a crucial factor in deciding whether to accept such an assertion is one's criterion of 'goodness'; yet very few of the defenders of 'good' schools have any clear criterion in mind, or, if they have, can guarantee that it is shared by many of their allies.

To some parents, 'goodness' would consist (perhaps most straightforwardly) in the production of a child who was religious or morally good in the old sense of *Anne of Green Gables*, for example. This, one suspects, is rare. Perhaps more commonly, it would consist in 'efficiency', particularly efficiency at securing satisfactory examination results or in providing a wide curriculum to what is regarded as a high academic standard. One mother, for example, was recently heard to say that she had chosen a certain private school for her son on the grounds that it offered Portuguese to university entrance standard, although she had no reason to believe he would ever study or be proficient in the subject; he was not quite five at the time. Another type of parent might simply see as a 'good' school one which, although providing reasonable academic training, would concentrate on making their child feel happy and wanted – in other words, almost completely the opposite in its emphases to the type of 'good' school seeking only examination successes and which, as a Sussex University lecturer said recently, may have its aims put in jeopardy if a student becomes too happy or contented.

However, given that the British schools most widely regarded as 'good' tend to be those attended by the children of the richer classes, one cannot escape the feeling that for a more realistic explanation of 'goodness' one must turn to the sociologist who sees in the threat to a 'good' school a threat to the seedbed of a particular social class, and to the values, myths and self-esteem which that class has built around itself. Anyone who has attended an English grammar or public school, unless he is an extreme revolutionary, can easily feel the pangs involved in the 'destruction' of something which he helped to form himself, however convinced he may be on rational grounds that such destruction is necessary. After all, even the public schoolboy who hated his school vehemently will blithely send his son there. Its socialising qualities may still seem to him snobbish, silly or even pointless, but the social grouping to which he belongs declare them to be 'good', and he is hard put to it not to go along with this.

Even more sociologically interesting, of course, is the belief among many who have never been there that high status boarding schools are 'good' because they 'traditionally' produce our leaders. The fact that four times as many Prime Ministers between 1900 and 1950 had been to day schools as to Eton seems lost upon them, though they are of course right in thinking that the majority of lesser ranking cabinet ministers and of the middle-rank officers in the Civil and Armed Services did go to those 'good' schools which left-wing politicians seem determined to destroy.

In any case, however, it is impossible to establish finally whether top people are produced as a result of what happens in a particular establishment, or because only top people enter that establishment in the first place. Equally, though one may argue that they would not go there in the first place if it did not offer something 'good', it may turn out that the 'goodness' may simply consist in mixing with other potentially top people and indulging in activities which they will later value highly. Whether such activities are in themselves 'good' judged against eternity is quite another question, and one which even Plato, the great inspirer of the modern élitist school, found it sufficiently difficult to answer.

Merely to assert or assume the 'goodness' of a particular school is, therefore, naïve, and gets us nowhere unless at the same time we are continually questioning wherein its 'goodness' lies. This is of course a truism of the traditional academic study of Education, but it does not necessarily prevent the education-alist from talking at one moment in sceptical philosophical terms of 'goodness' and 'success', and at the next moment talking quite glibly in quantified terms of 'better' results and 'more successful' methods, as if what is educationally desirable were perfectly obvious.

Such philosophical slackness would be laughable if its political consequences were not so grave for party decisions, whether in parliament or university senate, are all too often based on just such invocations of the 'obvious'.

Let us examine, for instance, the notion that the teacher is *in loco parentis* to his student. It is used, at school and university level, to justify the exercise by the teacher of a pastoral role rarely, if ever, exercised by teachers outside the English system or those modelled on it. In later chapters we discuss the nine-teenth-century growth of the notions of 'housemaster' and 'uni-versity tutor as pastor', but it is worth remembering that no such notion arose in Scottish universities or colleges until, in this century, the power of fashion made desirable those Ameri-can and English models of academic residence and student counselling and supervision which Scotland, like France, had hitherto avoided. Indeed, Scots and Scottish churchmen in par-ticular were extremely dubious about schools or universities undertaking any such tasks. They saw the role of the educational institution, when compared with the family, as severely and rightly circumscribed. They even saw its disciplinary role as restricted. Riots in the Old College of Edinburgh during the 1850s were serious enough to worry the French government, but were at first said by the professors to be no concern of theirs.

Nevertheless, a number of legal decisions (influenced heavily, one suspects, by the late-nineteenth-century beliefs of the English public school boy) have long since established the teacher's rights in Common Law as being *in loco parentis* – having a duty therefore to supervise the child's moral education and to punish his misdemeanours 'as a parent would'. Yet how *would* a parent? Is it possible to generalise? Do we not often mean that the teacher teaches and punishes as he thinks a parent *should*, were he not so feckless or misguided? One public schoolmaster went so far as to say that parents and their slackness were the biggest menace to supervision of his pupils' sex lives – they *would* let them meet girls and thus become 'unsettled' during the holidays! It is hard to see how he could really be described as *in loco parentis*, unless the phrase carries the assumption that, educationally speaking, the parent has taken on a secondary role, instead of being the principal educator, the decider and arbiter of educational policy, with the teacher as his mere agent. *In loco parentis* has come to mean displacing rather than temporarily replacing the parent.

In fact, we have long since thrown overboard even the merest pretence of the teacher as the parent's agent. Many headmasters are even chary about allowing parents about the place in case they embark on American-style interference in the running of the school. Talk of 'professionalism' in teaching has long since left the parents behind to such an extent that *in loco parentis* would just as aptly describe the surgeon or the dentist, performing tasks that the parents could never undertake or even supervise themselves.

This point has been pressed strongly because it is a typical instance of the way in which we have all become bamboozled by the use of educational catch-phrases for political purposes. Teachers, whether in school or university, chiefly use *in loco parentis* nowadays not as a reminder of duty to the student's family but to justify punishments or interferences in students' lives, about which parents' advice is rarely sought.

It is typical also that punishment is often seen not primarily to protect the child's interests but to safeguard 'the good name of the school'. On the other hand, if a student fails he is regarded as the culprit, rather than the teacher or institution who failed to train him properly. If the same pupil had done something praiseworthy the institution would have been the first to claim any credit. A professional solidarity has developed among teachers which demands subscription to the belief that teachers cause success, pupils cause failure. This is not the professional solidarity found among shopkeepers or doctors, who treat their failures either more guiltily (when it is their fault) or less ostentatiously when it is nobody's.

To some extent of course, this situation is the result of the nineteenth-century belief in the examination not merely as a test of memory or intellectual ability but of moral worth. As Jowett told the first Civil Service Commissioners:

For the moral character of the candidates I should trust partly to the examination itself. University experience abundantly shows that in more than nineteen cases out of twenty, men of attainments are also men of character. The perseverance and self-discipline necessary for the acquirement of any considerable amount of knowledge are a great security that a young man has not led a dissolute life.[1]

Thus the teacher who has failed to purvey the facts or inculcate the skills can, unlike the doctor, easily fall back on the incantatory assertion that the pupil has 'failed' through his 'laziness' just as, had he succeeded, the teacher could then have preened himself on 'helping to get him through'. This, of course, is to say no more than that teachers are human. Nevertheless, it might produce a greater earnestness of purpose if less cant surrounded this question of educational 'success' and 'failure'.

Professional mystique has seen to it that parents have a touching faith in the claims, reliability and validity of examinations. Some public attention is now being paid (although as yet within a very narrow circle) to questions of reliability – whether more than one examiner on more than one occasion would award the same candidate the same result. Hardly anything has yet been seen in the press, however, about the validity of examinations –

whether they really test the qualities or body of knowledge they claim to be testing. There is much talk of untested qualities such as 'originality' or 'creativity' (two terms much confused in usage), but then most examinations at school level are never meant to test them in the first place. They merely claim to assess the student's 'standard' in chemistry or his 'skill' at composition or mathematics. In fact, the testing of either involves frighteningly vast value-judgements. Who can tell whether the current standards of chemistry professors or the skills approved by 'expert' literary critics will not seem ludicrous in the light of history, as many of the skills and standards of earlier days now seem to us? May we not, in our current examinations, be rejecting those very pupils whose different but more insightful standards of chemical analysis or literary skills are destined to be highly valued in the distant future? We must, naturally, be pragmatic and establish some working standards, however temporary, otherwise selection in a competitive society becomes impossible; but at least we could try to be a little less arrogant about a process fraught with uncertainties.

Within such uncertain criteria of 'success' the examiner can as a rule quickly spot the certain successes and the certain failures. His problems arise over the borderline candidates who, as every conscientious examiner knows, are usually the majority. In order to resolve his problems he falls back on a base-line of pass/fail decided by others and blinds himself to the fact that he could not *really* discriminate between those with 48 per cent (fail) and 51 per cent (pass) unless he had artificially manipulated the marks in the direction in which he 'feels' they should go, so as to leave a candidate on one side or the other of an arbitrary line. After all, even if the standards of chemistry examinations were laid up in heaven, who can say that a man with 50 per cent (or, let us say, a 'C') should go out into the world with success stamped upon him by the world of chemists, while the man with 49 per cent (or 'D') goes out stamped a lifelong failure?

It is, of course, largely fruitless to discuss the use of such terms as 'pass' or 'failure' with most academics or teachers, because so much of their own self-esteem is bound up with a firm belief in their validity. It is therefore not surprising that most parents should still believe in them implicitly, and should continually be amazed at the lack of correspondence between examination results and their own assessment of the child's strengths and weaknesses.

Teachers, of course, retort that parents are hopelessly biassed and that examinations have 'objectivity' – another guarantee of 'standards' among academics. Yet a considerable body of psychological evidence has recently been built up which indicates that 'objectivity' is far more difficult to achieve in examining than was at one time imagined. The possibility of its erosion in the marking of so-called 'open-ended' essay-type answers is reasonably obvious. What is less obvious, but is now becoming clearer, is that even the setting of 'closed' answer items (multiple-choice and the rest) can involve cultural bias and linguistic pitfalls which make true objectivity extremely difficult to achieve – particularly in examinations mounted on a national or international scale, where no proper account can be taken of cultural differences between examiners and students, or between different groups of students.

Such difficulties underlie much of the discussion of different levels of 'intelligence' between races or sexes. It is extremely difficult, if not impossible, to construct tests that will take adequate account of the widely differing life experiences of the groups or individuals being tested. This is just one reason why no self-respecting psychologist would now claim that he is able to test a child's 'innate' intelligence. Indeed, he would be cautious about defining the term 'intelligence' itself, common though it is on the lips of those exercised over the future of 'good' schools.

In fact, we can as yet go little beyond the bare assertion that 'intelligence' is whatever quality an intelligence test *claims* to be testing. Thus, its meaning varies from tester to tester. At its most sophisticated, it may be testing behaviour which has been shown to predict other behaviour in areas of activity (such as examinations or mechanical aptitude) on which a high value is placed *by our particular society*. At its least sophisticated, as in the 'Brain of Britain' contest or 'University Challenge', it may be merely testing the possession of promiscuous scraps of factual information, the acquiring of which may or may not be related to some quality called 'academic ability' or 'intelligence'.

The assumption that a battery of tests called the 'eleven plus' or the unreliable marking of a set of essays can ever tell the truth about someone's 'intelligence' – let alone their worth as a human being or even their potential as a performer in a given situation – is perhaps the most dangerous made by our educational system. It has formed the basis for all kinds of highly dubious claims – that grammar schools and universities cater only for the 'best', the 'most intelligent'; that whites are 'more intelligent' (and therefore, by implication, superior) to blacks; that those with 'high intelligence' or 'high standards' will be 'dragged down' if allowed to mix with their inferiors.

The last of these recalls the Victorian insistence that rich children should not play with guttersnipes lest their manners and morals be corrupted. It is interesting to speculate on how those who would deplore such Victorian snobbery can justify educational separation based on levels of intelligence in what is still ostensibly (even legally) a Christian civilisation founded on belief in the basic equality of man.

The normal response to this jibe is, of course, that children are not being segregated as people but as 'intelligences', yet the emotive language generally used implies far more: the schools for the intelligent are 'good' schools (the others then by implication being 'less good' or even 'bad'), the children who go there are 'promising' (what is the implication of *that*?), the education provided there demands 'better' teachers (as if the best physicians are needed for the most healthy). All such frightening assertions are based on the assumption that we *have* valid and reliable ways of sorting the 'intelligent' from the 'unintelligent', the 'good' from the 'bad', when it is pretty clear that we do not. At least the Victorian snob could pretty reliably spot a guttersnipe when he saw one.

This emphasis on intelligence testing and the cult of the 'able' is of course very much a function of the way in which our society has developed over the last fifty years. A hundred years ago, universities and grammar schools were perfectly willing to accept whatever human material came their way. But with growing competition for entry into such institutions some criteria for selection had to be developed, however flimsy they later turned out to be. But during this period there has been an inevitable backlash. Indeed, for over a century the science of pedagogy itself has been influenced by a different set of forces, laying great emphasis on the rights of the individual child irrespective of his 'intelligence', and stressing the development of the individual personality rather than the interests of society. Schools sharing such beliefs are said to teach children rather than subjects, to encourage self-expression in the child and give him a considerable say in working out his own curriculum and even in the running of the school. There has also been an emphasis on the importance of learning by discovery rather than mere rote-learning of data regurgitated by a teacher taught in similar fashion. For want of a proper general term, those holding such views have been classed together as 'child-centred' or 'progressive'.

But the free and unexamined use of such terms is hardly fair to their opponents. The conventional grammar school headmaster could quite reasonably claim that by getting his 'good' pupils through the examinations required by society he is far more 'child-centred' than the irresponsible progressive who would allow a child to do no work and then cast him helpless at the age of eighteen into a competitive society placing a high value on formal qualifications. He would also be incensed that his school with its language laboratories, its student counsellors and its videotape machine should be labelled 'unprogressive'.

He would be equally justified in questioning his opponents' use of language. What, for example, do 'progressives' mean when they talk of 'developing the individual'? Do they mean that personal idiosyncrasies must be developed at all costs, that the teacher is *never* justified in adjusting the child, even against his wishes, to the needs of society (*i.e.* his fellow individuals)? If they believe *some* adjustment to be necessary, where do they draw the line without compromising their basic principles? And what do they mean by 'discovery-learning'? Must every child work unguided through the whole of human scientific discovery up to the present? Or do they really mean (as Rousseau clearly meant) that they should manipulate a child's learning without his being aware of it? This is surely at least as dangerous, and perhaps an even more sinister threat to individual freedom, than the more open (though bleak) authoritarianism of conventional, rote-learning classrooms.

The use of unexamined slogans and catch-phrases is not, then, confined to one type of educational or political thinking.

We are all emotionally involved in what educational institutions have done or failed to do for us, and therefore find it especially difficult to speak objectively of problems bound up with our deepest memories of childhood or adolescence. Science also has found it difficult to disentangle its educational findings from the scientists' own political and cultural assumptions about a field in which they themselves are deeply involved. (One of the supreme ironies in present-day academic life is the spectacle of serious psychologists solemnly marking essays on the impossibility of marking essays adequately.) The present writers both work in universities, which ought, according to the slogans, to guarantee a careful and judicious use of language. Yet they are already aware that in the following pages they are unlikely to escape all the pitfalls of educational discourse – the glib generalisations, the fashionable but inaccurate use of terms, the loading of arguments in favour of their own viewpoint. This proves only that educational argument is carried on by human beings; but, if education means anything, it means that human beings can learn to use their peculiar gift of complex language in a more accurate and useful way. It is highly desirable, therefore, that teachers, parents, students and politicians alike should learn to control themselves in educational argument. With this in mind, we hope that in the following chapters readers will increasingly find themselves taking us to task for using terms and slogans too loosely. To this end, we now append a list of words and phrases which we have not yet discussed, with some questions that might be asked about them:

Character-training: What is meant by 'training'? Training like a rose? Or a sea-lion? Can such a metaphor be aptly applied to organised interference in the actions of a free human being?

And what is meant by 'character'? Is it a collection of socially desirable characteristics – the character one loses on being convicted of a crime? Or is it the nonconformity discerned in the idiosyncratic person known locally as 'something of a character'? Is the process of 'character-training' a matter of securing conformity or fostering individuality? Is moral rectitude or creative ingenuity to be encouraged?

Study in depth: Is this the same as specialisation? Has an

English literature specialist who has read ten Shakespeare plays a deeper knowledge of them than a non-specialist who has read only *Lear* and *Hamlet* but has also studied history and psychology? Is 'depth' of study a different thing from 'width'? The cult of specialisation in the English sixth form seems to imply that it is not only different but also superior.

Academic success: In what sense is a student academically successful? In terms of his final examination mark, or in terms of the later application of his training to his work or life-style? Evidence suggests that success in a profession such as medicine is far from reliably forecast by examination performance. How academically successful is someone who gains a distinction in 'A' level French and never reads or speaks a word of French from that day onward? And how academically successful is the teaching which produced him?

Relevant studies: There seems to be a widespread belief that secondary schools would find it easier to motivate reluctant students if the curriculum were more 'relevant'. But relevant to what? To the student's current obsessions? To his eventual job? To his eventual hobbies? To his eventual marital problems? What if no relevant studies were possible? Should we then let him leave school before the age of sixteen? If not, how can we justify keeping him there if what he is doing is 'irrelevant'?

Curriculum: In discussing a 'relevant' curriculum, what do we actually mean by 'curriculum'? The syllabus, all the school's activities or only those on the time-table? Only those in the class-room? Or do we include games and 'encouraged' hobbies?

Do we mean what is said to happen or what the headmaster hopes is happening, or do we only mean what is *really* happening, as opposed to window-dressing? How do we discover or measure what is really happening?

Does a '*good education*' really produce a 'better' life? If so, in what sense, and by what criteria?

Middle-class values: What are they? Are middle-class pleasures and instincts different from others? Do middle-class people really think less about sport and sex and salaries than other people? Do they really have a greater interest in the arts and matters intellectual? If they do show such an interest, how far is it motivated by genuine interest and how far by outdated social conventions? Are there not dangers in forcing on children a curriculum embodying values which their parents no longer believe in, and perhaps never have?

'Schooldays are the happiest days of your life': Is this true? If so, why? If not, why not? What do such questions tell us about the values of our society? Can we justify an examination system which forces those of our citizens who are physically fittest and at their most responsive to natural beauty to spend the finest months of the year indoors and often in a state of acute anxiety?

'Children should be seen and not heard.' 'Spare the rod, spoil the child.' What do such proverbs tell us about those who utter them? Would 'arrogant', 'wise' or 'experienced' be suitable descriptions? How many of those who never use such expressions really believe them in their hearts? How does this affect their actual behaviour?

The list could be prolonged almost indefinitely, as could the questions. It is hoped that the following chapters will provide the opportunity for doing just that.

REFERENCES

1. Benjamin Jowett in a letter to Trevelyan, the inaugurator of the Civil Service reforms, quoted in W. J. Reader, *Professional Man* (Weidenfeld and Nicolson, London, 1966), p. 88.

CHAPTER THREE

LAWS OF NATURE AND TRIBAL CUSTOMS

'When I close my eyes,' says a character in one of Sartre's novels, 'the world ends.'[1] Not many go as far as that, but this cast of mind is not confined to tormented French intellectuals. Many primitive peoples regard themselves, if not as the whole human race, at least as its norm. Many nations' names for themselves mean simply 'the people' – Teutons, Bantu and Navajo are among the best-known examples. Ethnocentrism may concentrate on geography, as with the ancient Egyptians, who called their country 'the two lands' (*i.e.* Upper and Lower Egypt – the rest did not really count), or the modern Chinese, who still call their country *Zhongguo*, 'Middle Kingdom', the country at the centre of the world. Some peoples have concentrated on language, and characterised themselves as the 'articulate'; for example, Slav (and Slovak, Slovene, etc.) are cognate with *slovo*, a word; Euskara and Shqiperise – Basque and Albanian respectively – mean 'clear speech'. It works the other way too; witness *Hottentot* (stutterer), the Boers' name for the Khoikhoin people of Southern Africa or, to cite the best-known example, the Greeks' labelling of all non-Greeks as *barbaroi* (whence 'barbarians'), people who could not talk properly (*i.e.* Greek), but simply say 'bar-bar'. Not surprisingly, attitudes to political institutions are similar. Aristotle's celebrated definition of man as a 'political animal'[2] did not mean that he was particularly concerned with parties, votes and lobbies, but that it was in his nature to live in a *polis*, or city-state. He knew perfectly well, of course, that most men did nothing of the kind; but whether they were Scythian tribesmen or subjects of the Great King of Persia, they were 'barbarians' and, in political organisation as in language, less completely men.

Assuming one's own ways to be the norm is as common among modern industrialised nations as among primitives or ancients. 'Human nature', a distinguished American university president has written, 'is, always has been and always will be the same everywhere.'[3] Most people would probably agree with this, sweeping though it is. Of course, increasing culture-contact, especially since the nineteenth century, has brought more and more people up against the uncomfortable fact of variety over a vast range of human behaviour, making it more difficult to assume the normality of one's own pattern merely by default. But another time-honoured device can be brought into play. As the *Chanson de Rolland* has it, 'chretiens unt dreit e paiens unt tort' – Christians are right and pagans are wrong. Similarly, the Japanese regarded the Europeans who forced their way into their country in the nineteenth century as uncouth barbarians, the Christian missionaries in Polynesia recoiled in horror from native 'obscenity' (*i.e.* a recognition of and interest in sex), and so on. This has provided numerous occasions for quite genuine misunderstanding. A well-known semi-fictional example is the bewilderment of both Anna and the King of Siam at the other's view of the 'natural' relations between the sexes.[4] Bengt Danielsson provides another:

How alien the Christian view of sex life was to Polynesian ideas is well illustrated by the familiar anecdote about one of the first bishops in New Zealand. On a journey through his new diocese the bishop came one evening to a remote Maori village, where he was naturally received as befitted a guest of rank, with endless speeches and a huge banquet. When the bishop and the young clergyman who was his sole companion had endured the whole programme and were at last ready to retire for the night, the chief, according to good Polynesian custom, sent for a woman for the bishop. The young cleric, who happened to overhear the chief's order, stopped him and said indignantly:

'What do you mean? A bedfellow for the bishop?'

The chief could not imagine more than one explanation for this violent outburst of wrath and hastened to repair his error by shouting loudly to his servants:

'Give the bishop *two* women!'[5]

This kind of assumption is still widespread in what we are pleased to term civilised society. One of the most striking findings of Gorer's recent study of sexual habits in Britain was not merely the extreme variety reported in the frequency with which people had intercourse, but the fact that practically all the respondents believed that their own frequency was normal.[6]

Misunderstandings of this sort are not only liable to be highly charged emotionally; through the widespread habit of equating 'natural' with 'good', they are not infrequently given moral overtones as well. Thus, being different is not only abnormal, but pernicious. This is hardly surprising in such matters as sexual behaviour, where there is room for dispute and the rational formation of value-judgements – in principle at least, though less often in practice. But the heat is just as great – indeed, often greater – over matters where the value-content is not altogether apparent. A good example is the apoplectic response of many middle-aged people to the dress-fashions or hair-styles of the young. There are plenty of people solidly convinced that long hair is 'unnatural' on men, so much so that they claim to be unable 'to tell the boys and girls apart'. It is not clear why, in most circumstances, it is thought important that they should; in any case, those more directly involved, the young people themselves, do not seem to have any great difficulty – judging, at least, from the greater ease of personal and sexual contact against which the same critics, somewhat inconsistently, inveigh. But there is nothing new in this. In its own day, *short* hair was considered subversive, unnatural and even indecent, as witness the reaction to the 'croppy boys' of the eighteenth century. The now normal trousers were originally banned as indecent in many circles in the early nineteenth century;[7] so were trousers on women until much more recently, although (unless one cares to fall back on obscure quotations from Deuteronomy about transvestism)[8] it is hard to see what possible connection there is with morals either way. In our own day we are seeing a similar confusion over dress-lengths. Many people in our own society still regard exposure of the female breast as indecent, while in other cultures covering it is regarded as morally suspect, and in others again (the more traditional Muslim societies in particular) it is the *face* that must not be seen. Such objections are seldom expressed simply as personal preferences. There would be a case for this; one might even be able to have some sympathy with the headmasters who ban long hair one day and skinhead crops the next, as an understandable dislike of any evidence of the passing of his own youth. But this is not the way it is put; the assumption appears to be that deviation from one's *own* norm (usually the fashion of one's early adulthood) is not only personally unattractive but an offence against the right order of things. The very difficulty of establishing and justifying clear criteria seems to deepen the disapproval still further.

The wildest excesses are well publicised, but the frame of mind that gives rise to them is not confined to arbitrary headmasters or the dimmer town-councillors. Many intelligent and civilised people can find ethnocentrism difficult to shake off, in education as in other things. Nobody could call Sir Julian Huxley narrow-minded or insular; but this passage from his account of a visit to the Alafin of Oyo in Nigeria, during his service on the Elliot Commission on Higher Education in West Africa, suggests that even he seems to assume some kind of cultural package-deal, deviations from which, even when he is far too civilised to condemn them, are nevertheless seen as rather odd:

We then partook of a ceremony of friendship. We and the Alafin were given kola nuts on the back of our outstretched hands, a gesture which proved we were not holding concealed weapons; the nuts were then exchanged, and had to be chewed. They are very bitter, and contain a depressing and soothing alkaloid, which both promotes and symbolises non-aggression. I was fascinated to be plunged into this world of *barbaric ritual, so much in contrast with our ensuing discussion on higher education.*[9]

But why on earth should this 'barbaric ritual' be thought out of keeping with a discussion of higher education? We have a great many rituals, not dissimilar in form and practically identical in function; many a discussion of higher education is preceded by shaking hands and sipping a glass or two of sherry. On more formal occasions (in a university for example) participants put on fancy clothes that are not part of their normal dress, address each other by titles not normally used in conversation, and may even walk about preceded by a man in yet another kind of special dress carrying a stick with a big lump of metal on the end. Views of the desirability of such rituals vary, but they are not generally regarded as barbaric, nor is it often suggested that they are in contrast with the actual workings of the university or college. Some regard them as irrelevant, some as pleasant and harmless and some see them as part of the life and soul of the university itself. One set of rituals is familiar and therefore normal; the other is unfamiliar and therefore a barbaric tribal custom.

If this kind of thinking was confined only to the externals of the educational system it might not do much harm; it makes very little difference to the functioning of a university, after all, whether meetings of Senatus begin with prayer or whether the professors wear gowns or not. But the habit of generalising from one's own norms goes much further than that, to the structure, content, organisation and running of the educational process. The point at issue is not whether one's own practices are 'wrong' – they might turn out, on examination, to be quite appropriate. But the examination must take place for the approval to be worth having. As things stand, the equation of our own tribal customs with laws of nature rests much educational practice on a foundation of unexamined assumption which survives through default rather than merit.

A good example of this can be found in the age-structure of the educational process. Not the age of leaving school, perhaps; this has become too much a matter of change and controversy to be taken for granted. But beginning primary school at the age of five, moving on to a clearly-defined secondary stage at eleven or twelve, and thence to higher education at eighteen or thereabouts – this kind of sequence is widely assumed to correspond to clearly recognisable stages of development. The case for this particular segmentation is rarely argued. Occasionally one finds some rhetoric backing it up, as in the 1926 Hadow Report with its talk of 'a tide which begins to rise in the veins of youth at the age of eleven or twelve',[10] but rarely anything more precise. Not only do the Education Acts stipulate the division into primary, secondary and further education; nature itself is held to be the arbiter of the arrangement.

The historical and international picture gives less support than some might expect. In these islands, for instance, the very division between primary and secondary school, secondary school and university, is usually pretty blurred and generally recent. It is not so long since, for example, most of the universities were doing much the same kind of work as many secondary schools do now, or even did then. (We shall be looking at this more closely in Chapter 5.) The distinction between primary and secondary school is similarly of relatively recent creation. Indeed, in the independent sector it is still not on the same pattern; the normal age of transition from preparatory to 'Public' schools is not eleven, but thirteen, 'rising tide' or no. There is, of course, a transition to different *kinds* of study – foreign languages, for instance, or science, or mathematics – but the practice of the independent schools and their many imitators does not bear out the contention that this need involve a change of school at all, let alone a change combined with selection and allocation.

A glance at the organisation of other systems shows a rather different set of assumptions. Take the point of entry to formal schooling. Britain is almost alone in starting at the age of five. Most American states do not require attendance until six, which is also the beginning age in most European countries, such as France, Germany (East and West), Czechoslovakia and Hungary. Others begin still later: in Yugoslavia, the Soviet Union, Sweden and Switzerland the age of entry is seven. In most countries, certainly, a much higher proportion of pre-school children are in nursery schools – it can be over half, as in the USSR, over three-quarters, as in the USA, and in some cases nearly 100 per cent (as in France, Poland and Czechoslovakia). But this is not quite the same thing as beginning at five; as far as one can generalise, the predominant pattern is to introduce children to some kind of learning experience well before five (at the age of three to four, usually), but to postpone *formal* compulsory education to the age of six or seven. It seems to make very little difference in the long run as far as scholastic attainment is concerned.

Nor is there universal support for the practice of making a major break at eleven or twelve. The Americans do, though this simply means that all go on to the neighbourhood high school. The French do, though the selection and allocation process is spread over the four-year period from eleven to fifteen. Those West German states which still have selective systems make the break earlier, at the age of *ten*, on the assumption that it is not possible to have a reasonable secondary course if the selection is put off any longer. Most countries do introduce changes in the curriculum about eleven or twelve, such as the switch from general instruction by one class teacher to the teaching of distinct subjects by specialists. But this is usually an internal convenience, and is more and more being spread over a two- or three-year period. It does not involve anything like the major break in our own system, any more than in the independent sector. In Poland, Hungary and Yugoslavia the basic school covers an eight-year course, the major break coming at fifteen; in Denmark, Sweden and East Germany it comes at sixteen, after which there is some institutional differentiation. If any of these countries are 'missing the tide' which 'leads on to fortune', they seem none the worse for it; at any rate, the level of scholastic attainment is no less than that of English grammar school or Scottish senior secondary pupils. Most countries which do make the main transition at eleven or twelve have been moving away from it in the last few years. Against this background, our own system looks rather unusual. It *may* be none the worse for that, but at least it is not so easy to take it for granted as the only possible thing to do.

Again, it is still widely assumed that the assignment of children to particular groups or studies according to ability is an inevitable part of the educational process. There are differences, of course, over the stage at which this should start, over whether it should involve allocation to separate schools at some point, and so on. As usual, most people tend to take the particular variant in force in their own system at a given time as normal. Before 'non-streaming' gained ground in England, the majority of primary-school teachers were convinced that the division of children into clear-cut ability groups was unavoidable if the work of the school were to proceed.[11] In Scotland, where streaming has never been common at the primary stage, few teachers considered it, but assumed like their English colleagues that it was inevitable at the secondary stage. Many have gone so far as to argue that separate *schools* for the able are necessary to ensure reasonable academic progress, and, where comprehensive organisation has ruled this out, have sought to ensure the survival of clear-cut groupings within the comprehensive framework. In few cases, as we have seen, has there been much attempt to find out what actually happens anywhere else; yet even a brief survey of foreign practice shows that assumptions on this matter vary widely. In the USA, for example, there are usually completely unstreamed classes in the elementary school (up to age twelve), after which all go on to the local high school. There, a considerable variety of courses is available, but these are chosen by the students themselves, with guidance from full-time counsellors; they are not streamed in the British sense. In most East European countries children are taught in unstreamed classes up to the age of fifteen or sixteen, after which there is selection for theoretical or more practical courses. The Soviet Union goes rather further in having unstreamed classes throughout the general school; a minority leave at fifteen for more specialised schools of various kinds, but this is not the same thing as grading by ability. There are problems in this approach, such as the children at one end of the scale who find themselves repeating the year's work, and the highly gifted ones who find the general pace too slow; but the solution is sought through remedial teaching in the one case, and curricular enrichment through options or voluntary out-of-school classes in the other. None of this, of course, *proves* that selection or streaming are undesirable, but simply indicates that while some systems (*e.g.* in parts of West Germany) feel they need more of it than we do, others contrive to get by without it. Once again, a positive case has to be made; mere assumption will not do.

Another common form of ethnocentrism is the assumption that the only valid form of any type of education is that with which we happen to be familiar. Thus we find declarations about the nature of 'real secondary' work, and more particularly the 'real sixth form'. By these tokens, naturally, many developments in secondary education stand condemned – alteration of the balance of subjects, the admission of new (especially 'non-academic') material and, where it is thought to weaken the schools' efficiency in producing an academic élite, comprehensive schooling itself. Now it is perfectly reasonable to argue that the present mixture available in, say, an English grammar school has its points; many opponents of selection would agree, and some of them see comprehensive reorganisation as an opportunity to make it more generally available. But it is not reasonable to dismiss as 'not really secondary' anything which works out otherwise. 'Secondary' means nothing more than a second distinctive stage. There are many systems which organise the pattern of schooling differently anyway, and there are others (such as the United States) where the offerings in the high school are rather different from those of the grammar school. To argue that they are less desirable, or effective, or any other adjective one cares to apply, is a point of view. But it has to be argued; to dismiss the high schools of America as 'not really secondary' is, quite literally, meaningless. Coming after the primary schools, they are secondary by definition. Whether they are *good* secondary schools is an important, but separate, question – and one which, as we have seen, is not so easily resolved as appears on the surface.

The position of languages as a hallmark of 'real' secondary education is a case-study in itself. Before the Second World War, most English children did not go to secondary school at all, but completed elementary courses designed (mainly on nineteenth-century assumptions) to prepare them for work – hence the only recently departed rods, poles, perches, bushels and pecks, bills of sale and all that, with an eye to employment as shop-assistants, hostlers, drapers' assistants and the like. (Typically, the bushels and pecks survived the vanishing of horse-transport by decades.) Secondary schools of any kind had been for a minority, and were geared to the needs of entry to higher education, business, and some white-collar occupations. When 'secondary education for all' was eventually accepted in a changing climate of opinion, the upper end of the elementary school became the now familiar 'secondary modern'. To this day, it is a commonly held view that the 'true' secondary curriculum, including languages, lies within the compass of only an able minority. (The slightness of the language component in most American high schools is one of the features fixed upon by those who would deny them the title of 'real secondary'.) Now it may be arguable that not all older pupils need to learn a foreign language, but the experience of most European countries does not bear out the contention that it is impossible. In Germany, Scandinavia, the Netherlands, the Soviet Union and the East European countries, *all* children learn at least one; and in most of these countries, a substantial proportion study two or even three – more than are thought capable of learning *one* in Britain.

It is in higher education, however, that the temptation to take our current customs as the norm seems to be the strongest. Terms like 'real university' or 'university standard' are bandied about as regular ammunition in educational discussion; certain subjects are labelled as 'unworthy' of inclusion in the university curriculum, and so on. All too often, the argument is not whether a certain standard might, under present circumstances, be reasonable, or whether some subject might be more appropriately taught in some other kind of institution, or whether one kind of relationship with the state might be preferable to another; rather it is asserted that the very nature of a university demands in advance the answer to these questions. Thus, we find Lord James of Rusholme casting doubts on the claims of 'practical' subjects:

Unless we are prepared to face an alteration in our whole idea of a university and to justify its transformation into something altogether different, we may say that it is concerned with education at the spiritual level, using the word 'spiritual' to include the very highest intellectual activities. The university is concerned with studies aimed less at the skills of particular vocations than at the wisdom, that is to say, qualities such as judgement, the capacity and will to make new ventures in thought, and an interest in the perennial problems of man and society.[12]

Many have agreed with him, in spite of the difficulties raised by the obvious strength in the universities of such overtly vocational faculties as medicine and law. In fairness, James himself recognises this, but manages to get round it, while clinging to the general principle. He argues that in the case of medicine, its vocational narrowness is offset by other considerations:

Actually, however, when we consider the range of studies involved in a thorough and successful study of medicine – ranging as they do, or should, from psychology to biochemistry – when we remember the adequacy of the challenge that medicine can make to the best brains, and the remarkably wide front on which research is possible, we need have no misgivings about the legitimacy of the instinct which has made medicine one of the schools of longest standing.[13]

But the barrier is still brought down against other disciplines, at least as far as the universities are concerned:

Engineering gives rise to more serious doubts, and even if we accept the complete field of study included in the word, it is difficult to believe that specialised branches of engineering are suitable as complete degree courses ... Although, in my opinion, a number of the subjects usually called technical or vocational should be excluded from the universities, this is not to deny their great importance. They will actually be better served by encouraging new kinds of technical college to carry them on ... in which high standards are preserved by a loose affiliation with a university.[14]

Thus, years before the term 'binary system' had been coined, James articulated some of the major differences widely held to separate essentially the universities from other forms of higher education, notably the preference for general principles as against vocational skills, a concentration on the ablest élite, and concern for the pursuit of research. Some have carried several of these points rather further. A few have tried to fix on a particular *sine qua non*, like the Edinburgh professor who, echoing Newman,[15] recently insisted that no university lacking a faculty of divinity could be worthy of the name. The pursuit of excellence is a favourite. James, recognising that the concept is rather vague, contents himself with demanding that university study 'shall extend fully the intellectual capacity of the most intelligent men and women'.[16] Others are less inhibited by difficulties of definition. Sir George Pickering, for example, convinced that 'the objectives of university study should be the same, whatever subjects are chosen for study', puts his position thus:

University undergraduate education, be it for three or four years, should aim at honours standard. The student should know how to ask simple questions which admit an answer; to find original material relevant to the question and its answer; to arrange the material to form a judgement. This is the accepted method of 'training the mind'.[17]

A. J. P. Taylor went still further in his wrathful reaction to the Robbins Committee's expansion proposals in 1963, saying that the only people capable of benefiting from a university education were those capable of taking first-class honours degrees;[18] he did not, however, attempt to define those. Incidentally, one example of the faith in the universities' unique concern with high standards can be seen in James' suggestion that a university link with technical colleges could maintain standards even in subjects in which he feels the universities have no competence. At this point, one begins to suspect that many people's attachment to university standards is purely mystical.

Finally, universities are sometimes defined according to their relationship with the state; they are independent, whereas other types of college are liable to state control of one kind or another. The Minister who coined the term 'binary system'[19] made this one of the major criteria, but some have erected it into an absolute principle. Thus Lester Smith:

Our universities are outstanding examples of our belief in academic freedom ... Nor has there been any encroachment into university affairs by the state ... The universities now get about two-thirds of their money from the state ... yet they are completely self-governing ... How have they managed to maintain this freedom unimpaired? Tradition partly accounts for it. The older universities have their roots deep in the past ... They have grown from within.[20]

Or, once again, Sir George Pickering:

Academic freedom has always been, and always will be, an important principle in universities, particularly as expressed against the domination of Church and State. (Oddly enough, Oxford and Cambridge were exclusively Anglican from the Reformation until the nineteenth century.) In essence, it means the freedom to entertain and express an idea believed to be true, to teach according to these ideas, and to experiment on problems believed to be interesting.[21]

Whether most of these statements describe a real university that exists here and now, or has ever existed here, we shall be discussing in Chapter 5, though it is worth noting, in passing, that Pickering's remark about Oxford and Cambridge being exclusively Anglican seems more than somewhat at odds with the rest of his statement. For the moment, however, it may be useful to look around and consider how far the universities of other countries qualify as 'real'.

Right away, it becomes clear that although most other systems do make some distinction between universities and other kinds of institutions, they make it in different ways. In the USSR, for instance, the universities' relations with the state are exactly the same as those of other institutions – they all come under the control (in considerable detail) of the USSR Ministry

of Higher and Secondary Specialised Education. Their functions, certainly, are different. Most professional training is provided not in the universities but in other specialised institutions
of comparable level, and this includes not only engineering,
technology and agriculture, but such 'traditional university disciplines' as medicine and law. The role of the universities is
limited to what is left, that of providing courses in the pure
sciences and the humanities. Some of the graduates become research workers, but the majority join their counterparts from
the pedagogic institutes (teacher training colleges) teaching in
the secondary schools. The universities are thus left with a
rather small share of the higher educational system – 7·3 per
cent of the total student body and 7·9 per cent of the graduates,
as compared with the technical institutes, which have 44·1 per
cent of the students and 38·1 per cent of the graduates.[22]

Now it is true that in spite of official 'parity of esteem' the
universities do enjoy greater prestige than many other types of
establishments, and it is possible to interpret the figure given
above to mean that the students are of rather higher calibre. But
it is by no means clear-cut; although the most distinguished
handful of higher educational institutions in the country are
universities, many other institutions, notably some of the technical institutes, have a higher repute than many of the universities. Nor have the universities any particular monopoly of research; this is pursued in various types of higher institution,
and although the universities do much distinguished work they
are not the peak of the research pyramid. This role is reserved
for the scientific research establishments, which are quite separate, and in which nearly half the post-graduate students are
working for their higher degrees.[23]

To an extent, other European countries show similar de-
partures from what the British tend to see as the normal pattern.[24] In Germany, for example, the universities have to share
their pedestal with the *Technische Hochschulen*, or higher
technical institutes, while in France the professionally-oriented
Grandes Écoles, with their more rigorous entrance requirements
and tougher courses, tower over the universities in esteem. In
Germany, as in the USSR, the universities are generally up-
staged in research by specialised establishments. As for the
teacher training colleges, these are in Scandinavia at least rather

more difficult to get into than the universities.[25] Examples could be multiplied indefinitely, but it appears that in Europe at least the allegedly inherent distinguishing features of the university have no general validity.

In the United States, higher educational institutions differ enormously – in standard, prestige (not necessarily the same thing), size, relationship to the state, relationship to a church – but defy all attempts to separate out the 'real universities' by any clear criteria. We shall be taking a closer look at the question of size in Chapter 4, but we cannot expect to find this connected with 'quality' (whatever that means). Whether one is looking for large numbers as a sign of viability or small numbers as a sign of exclusiveness, the figures give no help either way.

Relationship to the state does not help much either. Tempting as it may be to look for private control as the touchstone of the 'real' university, the evidence does not support it, unless (like Humpty Dumpty)[26] we care to make the definition suit the evidence, which could produce some very odd results. It is of course true that some of the academically distinguished universities, such as Yale, Harvard, Princeton or Columbia, are private, but so are some of the worst. On the other hand, the state universities do include some mediocre establishments, but also some which are justly famous and can hold their own with the Ivy League or Europe – Michigan, Texas and California are probably the best known. Many of the private institutions are more prestigious socially, but this does not necessarily tell us anything about academic standards; some of them are little more than finishing schools, and do not pretend to be anything else. Incidentally, independence from state control is no guarantee of 'academic freedom', however that is defined; a Board of Trustees (businessmen, for the most part) can be just as interfering as any state governor, and less accountable.

The most obvious difference between the American set-up and our own is that there is no attempt to insist on a uniform 'university standard'. They hardly could, given the variety and looseness of the system, but that is not the point – they do not see why they should. Europeans still tend to insist that higher education, and universities in particular, must by their very nature concern themselves with an able minority (though how small this minority should be seems less readily agreed). The

Americans, however, do not see why this should be so, any more than at the secondary stage. This may result in having 'good' and 'bad' universities, with all the intermediate qualities. Such a system may have its defects – it can give rise to a good deal of practical confusion, for example – but it does not follow that only the 'good' ones can be recognised as universities at all, even if one could agree on what 'good' meant – unless, once again, we care to fall back on Humpty Dumpty definitions.

The greatest myth of all, perhaps, is that universities can be defined as places where pure learning, as opposed to vocational preparation, is pursued, and that this is what gives them their prestige. We have already seen the difficulties that James experienced in trying to find a justification for medicine within this conceptual framework, and how little the alleged pure/applied dichotomy has to do with the prestige of institutions in other countries. Engineering is a highly regarded profession in the USSR, France and Germany, and consequently the institutions which train engineers can hold their own with the universities. Business is well thought of in the USA, therefore the Harvard School of Business is not thought to sully the standing of that university, though it is hard to see how the intellectual content of that field can be regarded as intellectually richer than, say, the training of teachers. In Britain, the United States and many European countries, medicine and law enjoy a high level of esteem, and are readily catered for in the universities with very few qualms about their academic respectability. The universities have, in fact, been essentially vocational schools since their inception – medicine, civil and canon law and the higher levels of the priesthood in earlier times, scientific research, technology, economics and business more recently. If there are any criteria by which these disciplines can be regarded as more demanding than, say, education or art, they have yet to be convincingly stated. The correlation between the status and earnings of particular professions and the regard in which their feeder schools are held is much more obvious. The 'learned' professions – that is, those catered for in the universities – are those which got in earlier in the act. Some systems, like the American and the Soviet, have managed to adapt so as to allow for changing professional patterns; others, like our own, by insisting on a clear-cut qualitative division, obscure the issue by maintaining an essentially mythical picture. It may well be that there is a case for some kind of institution devoted to the disinterested pursuit of pure knowledge; but the universities do not fill this role, here or abroad, and never have done.

Another characteristic greatly prized by certain types of institution, and which is thickly encrusted with myth is independence. In later chapters we shall be examining this question more closely, especially in relation to British universities and secondary schools. It is striking, for instance, how often it is asserted that 'independence' from the state has always characterised the 'best' schools and colleges. Lester Smith, speaking of schools, disposes of this one firmly:

Those who sometimes speak as if schools today are in chains as never before and suggest that there was once a golden age of freedom will not find medieval administrative practice helpful to their argument ... Such autonomy as the medieval schools enjoyed was ... always subject to the absolute authority of the Church. The most effective instrument of control was the Bishop's licence to teach, a device to ensure that all who taught were loyal to the doctrine of the Church ... Eton masters had to take an oath not to 'favour the opinions, damned errors or heresies of John Wycliffe ... under pain of perjury, and expulsion ipso facto.'[27]

He usefully reminds us that there are other kinds of control than that crudely exercised by the state; and, of course, when the English Reformation turned the Church into an arm of government, Church and state control usually came to the same thing anyway – we have already seen that in Tudor times the Privy Council did not hesitate to interfere in anything from a teacher's religious views to the Latin grammar book which he used.[28] In Scotland, where the Reformation involved the establishment of a theocratic state rather than a state-run church, the effects could be similar, with all teachers having to submit to a Church-run licensing system. (This requirement lasted right up to 1861.)

However, there can be little doubt that in present-day Britain the independent sector does, rightly or wrongly, enjoy a greater social, and to some extent academic, prestige that the publicly provided sector. But there is nothing innate or inevitable about this. In the USA, for example, about 15 per cent of all pupils go to private schools (far more than most Americans realise, and a higher proportion than in Britain).[29] This is not to say that these schools are more outstanding academically or socially. Some of them are, such as the 'preparatory' schools in New England, but the great majority are denominational schools, mostly Catholic. Religious teaching in schools is not allowed in the USA (a recent Supreme Court decision ruled it to be unconstitutional); accordingly, parents who want a religious-based education for their children have to seek it outside the system. The same is broadly true of France[30] which, although predominantly Catholic, is a secular state, and state schools do not teach religion. Time is left for children whose parents wish it to have instruction provided by the Church, but those who want more than this – such as a curriculum based on Church teaching – have to go to Church schools for it. About 10 per cent do this, much more in areas like Alsace-Lorraine and Brittany. It would be quite wrong, however, to see these schools as anything like an élite, academic or social. On the contrary, the Church schools are generally considered less effective than the state schools, even after an injection of some public money under the Gaullist government. The really prestigious school is the *lycée*, a selective state-run secondary school with an exhaustive academic programme. In West Germany, likewise, the independent schools, which are mainly experimental, do not dominate the system; the most sought-after secondary school is the *Gymnasium*, a state-controlled school taking pupils from ten to nineteen or beyond. Incidentally, it is true that in France state control does mean close supervision of the work of the *lycée* (as of other schools), but this, while possibly irksome, cannot be said to lower standards. But even this degree of control does not necessarily follow; the German state *Gymnasien* are left with a considerable degree of initiative. Nor does this usually mean, as it so often does in England, the dictatorship of a headmaster instead of one of the LEA. Once again, there are many kinds of independence, and different kinds of control. The fact that a school is 'independent' does not, of itself, tell us a great deal in this country, and even less in the world at large.

Generalisation from one's norm is frequently applied to the content of education as well as its form. Consider the grammar school, and especially the sixth form. The 'sixth', in which pupils from the age of sixteen or so specialise in two or three cognate subjects to the Advanced Level of the GCE, is the pride and joy of many headmasters. It is popular, too, with the teachers, at any rate with those who teach at this level, and with the universities, which are able to use 'A' level work as the basis of further specialised study. It is true that the standard thus gained in individual subjects is of a high order, making schools using this system particularly suited to preparation for the universities as at present ordered. Robin Davis, a leading defender of the grammar schools, puts it thus:

Grammar schools have always served as a bridge to the university, though not all pupils crossed it ... Always, however, their aim has been a high standard of intellectual attainment, and this has been self-perpetuating ... Two practical effects of this tradition of scholarship are very much in evidence today. The academic standards of these schools make possible shorter university courses in Britain than elsewhere, and their former pupils, especially in the sphere of science and technology, are much in demand through having had a head start on pupils of the same age in other countries – hence the so-called 'brain-drain'.[31]

Davis does not mention sixth-form specialisation specifically at this point, but it is implicit in what he says about grammar-school scholarship. Actually, many of his statements are questionable. The use of 'always' invites closer inspection of the past record, as we shall see in Chapter 6. His remarks about the shortness of university courses apply to England rather than Britain (the Scottish honours courses take four years), and although some countries do have university courses of five years or more, others have four (Germany and the USA, for instance), and some three (e.g. France and some courses in Scandinavian universities). Not that three-year courses are self-evidently a good thing; if they are as highly specialised as in England, and even more if they take off from highly specialised school courses, the price may well be thought too high. The assertion about a 'head start' is also dubious – does this mean in one or two subjects, or in general educational attainment? It is certainly not so if the latter is meant. The English sixth-former is academically ahead of the American High School graduate (though we have seen some of the limitations of this kind of comparison); but it would be rash, and unsupported by evidence, to claim a similar advantage over the holder of the Soviet *attestat*, the German *Abitur*, the French *baccalauréat* or the Danish *studentereksamen*. The last three, indeed, are generally reckoned to be above the 'A' level; or rather, they are at about the same standard subject for subject, but maintain this over six to eight subjects instead of two or three. Specialisation is, of course, one possible approach to 'scholarship', but the more generalist approach of the Continental schools shows that it is not the only one, nor necessarily the most effective. Incidentally, the 'brain drain' phenomenon was far more complex than Davis allows, and was never in any case as general as he suggests. It was, in fact, largely a function of academic and industrial expansion in North America and Australia. Other industrial countries, such as France and Germany for instance, had little need to attract talent from Britain. It may simply have been that British employers and universities were more parsimonious than other countries in the western world. This purely financial explanation is reinforced by the considerable restriction on the 'brain drain' following economic retrenchment in North America.

Moral education is another area where ethnocentric mythology is strong. There is a vast amount of woolly thinking on the subject, hopelessly entangled with questions concerning the place of religion in the schools. Since 'indoctrination' always seems by definition to be something that other people do, the arguments brought forward to support the teaching of Christian doctrine in the schools (non-denominational only *within* the Christian context, not outside it) are often of a cultural nature – 'Christianity has had an important part to play in our civilisation', 'This is still a Christian country', etc. While the second of these statements is open to argument – the Humanist Association is at present collecting embarrassing statements to the contrary from figures as diverse as Mr Malcolm Muggeridge and the Archbishop of Canterbury[32] – the first is acceptable enough. It is hard to see, however, how this can be used to justify the requirement of 'a daily act of corporate worship'. It is not, after all, thought necessary to make children attend animal sacrifices and reading of the omens to help them understand Greco-Roman mythology, which has also had a marked impact on

European culture. Now, a case can be made by Christians (or Muslims, Jews, Parsees or whatever) for seeking to propagate their beliefs through schools or any other means available. If one believes that a particular brand of faith is essential for personal salvation, it is quite logical to see it as one's duty to bring others into the fold for their own good or, as the man in the parable put it, 'Go out, and compel them to come in.'[33] It is not an argument that has much force with those who take a different view, of course, but it is only in recent times that this has been much of an inhibition to those who *knew* the truth. Enforcing 'true' belief for people's own good is not a popular position, but it has the merit of consistency.

But this is not the way it is put. Not only is there confusion between teaching religion and teaching *about* religion, there is a further confusion between religion and morality. One of the commonest arguments for the retention of religion in schools is that it is essential for the child's moral development. A recent poll,[34] which suggests a general acceptance of the present position by a majority of parents, also shows that this is the kind of consideration they had in mind.

Naturally, a religious creed is one possible basis for a moral code, and an acceptable one to the extent that one holds the dogma to be true. But it is quite fallacious to insist that it is the only possible one; in fact, a great many countries do without it, while still conducting moral education in their schools. With the exception of the denominational schools, American schools are forbidden to teach religion. It might possibly be argued that the present level of crime, juvenile delinquency and allied problems are not a good advertisement for this practice, but two points have to be made before jumping to conclusions. First, it so happens that church membership and attendance are much more widespread than in this country, so that the churches must be held, on this argument, to be falling down on the job. Second, as we have seen earlier, the social problems of the USA are much too complex to admit of such simple connections with school experience. It *could* be argued that moral education in the USA has failed; but to argue that it has failed because it is non-religious requires much more evidence. In the communist countries, religious education has no place in the school programme at all. (Some of them allow it on a voluntary basis outside regular school hours.) Moral education nonetheless is an important function of the schools; it is based on Marxism-Leninism (or its Maoist variant in China), on social rather than on theological values. There are times when the approach to Marxism carries many of the overtones of religion, especially in its more dogmatic phases. But a fundamental difference remains: good and bad, right and wrong, are defined in terms of social effect, not in relation to a divine will. Not too much should be made of the *relatively* low level of serious crime or delinquency; there is not much evidence, either way, to connect social behaviour with the kind of moral education received in the schools – too many other factors are involved. France also has a secular system, and once again the evidence is ambiguous. Interestingly enough, in the Scandinavian countries, where the present moral climate is particularly repellent to many of the religious lobby in this country (including some moderate opinion as well as the 'Festival of Light' brigade), religious education *is* part of the normal school programme. When one remembers that it is prominent in the schools of Northern Ireland also, one might be tempted to discern a *harmful* effect. But once again, the issue is too complex for that. There is no convincing evidence to lay the blame for bigotry in Ireland, repression in Spain, environmental pollution and corruption in Italy (or, for that matter, 'permissiveness' in Scandinavia) at the door of religious education. Nor is there evidence to bear out the contention that religion is a necessary basis for moral education. The question is still open, and the case for teaching a particular doctrine (for that is what it amounts to) is yet to be made.

More generally, most of what is taught in the schools has an air of inevitability about it; many people manage to believe that the curriculum is both traditionally sanctioned *and* logically thought through. Not a great deal needs to be said about the traditional basis. A great deal of the material is much more recent than is often supposed; much of it was put there for an originally quite different purpose (Latin, once the international language of scholarship, was an obviously practical subject), rather in the way some teachers now justify wearing gowns because it keeps the chalk off their clothes. The very theory underlying educational tradition is, as often as not, misinterpreted. For generations, educational traditionalists have tended to use the name of Plato to justify a highly theoretical, even classical, curriculum, in which the practical, aesthetic and physical subjects have been regarded as at best peripheral. As true Platonists like Jowett were aware, although Plato did set a high value on theoretical study, and looked with some suspicion on practical training, what he actually advocated was mathematical rather than literary in nature, and this took place at what we would now regard as the higher educational stage. His equivalent of the school course *was* literary, but also artistic and physical; one wonders what he would have made of forcing children into the grammatical study of foreign languages and the rigidity and value-systems of team games – many of which were originally intended, educationally speaking, as a means of encouraging *esprit de corps* and submerging the individual.

A discussion of such issues is also a useful reminder that even the basic elements of the curriculum are not necessarily immutable. Reasonably enough, we tend to regard the skills of literacy and numeracy as fundamental as, in our particular society at this particular stage, they are. In Plato's day, memorisation, talking, running, jumping and fighting were basic;[35] among Margaret Mead's Samoans,[36] child-minding and weaving, canoeing and fishing, gardening and sex were more important. Literacy, in mediaeval Europe, was a special skill of the clergy; for the underprivileged peasantry, as for the privileged nobility, other matters loomed larger, such as ploughing and harvesting in one case, and weapon-skill, horsemanship and heraldry on the other. This does not mean that anyone is necessarily wrong, but simply that even in such a matter as the basic skills of the educational process, one's assumptions and familiar practices turn out, after a closer look, to be peculiar to one's own particular circumstances. Once again, they may be none the worse for that, and examination may lead to their abandonment, modification or confirmation. But this cannot be done until the assumption is dropped that they are necessary or inevitable; even the good points of one's tribal customs cannot be accurately appreciated if they are persistently confounded with natural law.

REFERENCES

1. Mathieu Delarue in *Les Chemins de la liberté*.

2. Aristotle, *Politics*.

3. Vice-President Hutchins, University of Chicago, *Fortune*, June 1943.

4. Rogers and Hammerstein, *The King and I*.

5. Bengt Danielsson, *Love in the South Seas* (Hulton, 1958), p. 31.

6. Geoffrey Gorer, *Sex and Marriage in England Today* (Nelson, 1972).

7. Gillian Edwards, *Uncumber and Pantaloon* (Geoffrey Bles, 1968), p. 9.

8. Deuteronomy, 22:5.

9. Julian Huxley, *Memories* (Allen and Unwin, 1970), pp. 268–9. (Emphasis supplied).

10. See Chapter 1.

11. *E.g.* Brian Jackson, *Streaming: An Educational System in Miniature* (Routledge and Kegan Paul, 1964).

12. Eric James, *An Essay on the Content of Education* (Harrap, 1949), pp. 64–5.

13. *Ibid.*, pp. 68–9.

14. *Ibid.*, p. 69.

15. Newman, *The Idea of a University*.

16. James, *op. cit.*, p. 67.

17. George Pickering, *The Challenge to Education* (Penguin, 1969), p. 92.

18. *Sunday Express*, October 1965.

19. Anthony Crosland.

20. W. O. Lester Smith, *Education: An Introductory Survey* (Penguin, 1957), p. 166.

21. Pickering, *op. cit.*, p. 121.

22. Raw figures from the official statistical yearbook. *Narodnoe khozyaistvo SSSR v 1969 godu* (Moscow, 1970).

23. *Ibid.*

24. See, *e.g.* Edmund King, *Education and Development in Western Europe*, (Addison and Wesley, 1969), and W. D. Halls, *Society, Schools and Progress in France* (Pergamon, 1965).

25. Universities admit anyone with the school-leaving examination, whereas the teachers' colleges are selective.

26. 'When *I* use a word,' said Humpty Dumpty, 'it means whatever I choose it to mean, no more and no less.' Lewis Carroll, *Alice through the Looking-Glass*.

27. Lester Smith, *op. cit.*, p. 128.

28. See Chapter 1.

29. US Office of Education Figures.

30. W. R. Frazer, *Education and Society in Modern France* (Routledge and Kegan Paul).

31. Robin Davis, *The Grammar School* (Penguin, 1967).

32. *Humanist News*, October 1971, p. 4.

33. Luke, 14:23.

34. The survey, conducted by National Opinion Polls (*New Society*, May 1965) showed 90 per cent of parents favouring the present system. The British Humanist Association, complaining that the NOP poll gave insufficient choice and confounded belief with morality, conducted its own poll and came up with results much less favourable to the teaching of religious belief (*New Society*, 24 April 1969). On a similar point, two American researchers have found no correlation, one way or the other, between lack of religious belief and juvenile delinquency (Travis Hirschi and Rodney Stark, *Social Problems* Vol. 17. No. 2, p. 202, reported in *New Society* 4 June 1970).

35. Plato, *The Republic* (Parts III and VIII in the Penguin edition, 1963).

36. Margaret Mead, *Coming of Age in Samoa* (Penguin, 1943).

CHAPTER FOUR

THROUGH THE LOOKING-GLASS

Ever since Solomon urged the sluggard to study the ways of the ant, using evidence from one field of study to bolster up arguments in another has been a popular rhetorical device. Men have been exhorted to virtue, or constrained to avoid vice, through lessons drawn from the animal kingdom, from the doings of their ancestors, from the ways of other peoples, with a persistence that resists prosaic objections that the illustrations owe less to accuracy than the desire to make a point.

At least the authors of the mediaeval bestiaries knew what they were doing. The whale was said to lie motionless like an island, wait for mariners to land on its back, then plunge into the depths and leave them all to drown. That whales had never been known to do this was not the point; the authors were not concerned with natural history, but with morality, and wanted a vivid illustration of the devil's temptations for the unwary. The ant is held up as an example of industry and foresight, as in Solomon before and La Fontaine after, but with the additional emphasis on laying up spiritual credit. The snake sloughs its skin as a symbol of spiritual rebirth, the mermaid tempts sailors on to the rocks (with an obvious moral), and in each case the lesson is more important than the facts. In some cases no attempt has been made at accurate description; the panther, for instance, is a beautiful animal, black with white spots, 'there is none fairer in this world'; he goes to sleep after eating, sleeps soundly for three days, then rises on the third; he breathes a sweet smell that spreads everywhere, so that 'every animal that hears him comes to him and follows him ... because of the sweetness that I have told you of', except for the dragon. The explanation makes it clear that this has nothing to do with panthers, but that 'Christ is signified by this beast', the three days' sleep and the awakening stand for the Crucifixion and Resurrection, the sweet smell for the Gospel, and the dragon for the Devil.[1] At a time when it was generally assumed that creatures with no obvious use to man (such as food or labour) were made specifically to instruct him,[2] pedagogic distortion of this kind must have seemed quite reasonable; if the facts did not fit the lesson, so much the worse for the facts.

Nor is this an exclusively ancient or mediaeval approach. Pictures like the *Stag at Bay* (bravely defending its trusting family from a pack of ravening wolves) had little to do with the behaviour of stags but fitted neatly with the self-image of the Victorian paterfamilias in whose drawing-rooms they hung. Modern nature fiction abounds in examples of harmonious home-life in birds' nests, loyal and self-sacrificing dogs and horses, and so on. Not many have tried to go as far as 'singing woodman' Seton Thompson, who wrote a book to prove that all living things obeyed the Ten Commandments (he had a good deal of trouble with adultery and gave up completely over swearing and Sabbath-breaking, understandably enough),[3] but the accounts of group loyalty among elephants and baboons and Disneyesque versions of bird courtship suggest a continued popularity of the anthropomorphic or at least anthropocentric approach. If close observation disturbs the cosy picture, this can be used too; the work of Lorenz, Morris and Goodall has exploded a whole battery of zoological myths from the peacefulness of doves[4] to the cowardice of hyenas,[5] but at least one author has used similar material to back up hierarchic society and private enterprise economics (Robert Ardrey),[6] while another, Sally Carrighar, has suggested that human sexual guilt has a biological origin – guilt, apparently, at mating out of season.[7]

As with the brute creation, so with people. Holding up noble ancestors as a reproach to degenerate descendants has always been a popular trope, but improvements in documentation has made this more difficult than it was in Livy's day.[8] (Many school textbooks, however, being free of such inhibitions, still carry on with it.) Likewise, we have come a long way since Rousseau's noble savage shamed upper-class mothers into taking more interest in their children, but anthropologists still have occasion to complain about the extrapolation of half-considered versions of their own findings to quite different conditions in industrial societies. One does not have to be quite so fanciful as Othello to mythologise about other cultures, when even nations which have been our neighbours for centuries are still seen in stereotypes; a recent poll in Britain suggested that the French, for instance, are seen as being 'too interested in sex',[9] which must give all the analysts of Britain's swinging permissive society something to think about. Perhaps the liking for familiar points of reference encourages Englishmen to think of the French as dirty and sexy, the Scandinavians as clean and sexy (as well as being suicidal), the Latins as emotional and the Teutons as ruthlessly efficient, the Scots as mean, the Welsh as dishonest and the Irish as drunk, but it is a dangerous line of thought nonetheless. The French and the Swedes, the Scots and the Welsh can look after their own images, but the Englishman who uses stereotypes to shore up his conviction of his own normality and rightness is doing himself no service. 'See how awful and/or funny they are – they're different from me' may be comforting, but hardly conducive to understanding oneself or others; both are obscured by mythical perceptions.

This happens with education too. With the improvement of communications we have progressed beyond both the Eldorado and 'here be dragons' world view, but are still inclined to pay attention to what other people are doing only in so far as it serves to support arguments about our own activities, either as shining examples of what we ought to be doing or, more often, as awful warnings of the way we are going. There are two difficulties in this approach: in the first place, conditions may be so different that the comparison is invalid, for good or ill; and secondly, we often manage to get it wrong anyway.

Among the controversies in which arguments from other systems have been pressed into service are the expansion of higher education (which is said to have produced massive impersonal degree factories with low standards in America, and anarchy in France); student participation in university government (which is said to have given rise to political turmoil in Latin America); 'progressive' teaching methods, especially in primary schools (for which we are to blame low standards and violence in America, and moral corruption in Scandinavia); and comprehensive education (which has produced low-level work in America and denial of individual differences in Russia, with such bad results that in both countries they are returning to more selective systems.)[10] Let us start by looking at the last of these.

It must be said right away that there is nothing wrong with looking to other systems for ammunition in the argument; it is only sensible, if we are reorganising along comprehensive lines, to see how similar systems have worked out elsewhere, with due regard for differences of context. Unfortunately, this very necessary qualification is frequently disregarded, with some odd results.

Since both the USA and the USSR are tolerably well known to have operated large-scale comprehensive systems for some time, it is natural that they should be looked to for evidence; and since they are also known to have large-scale problems, it is not altogether surprising that they are referred to most often by opponents of comprehensive schooling. With respect to the USA, the argument centres on the academic standards of the comprehensive high school where 'their seventeen-year-olds do not equal English fifteen-year-olds' or, as one British observer, the parent of a high school student, has put it:

> The only way a comprehensive non-selective system for all can work is to provide education that everyone can achieve, so that everyone, brilliant and dull alike, has an equal chance to succeed. This can only be achieved by lowering the standards to, at the very highest, the mediocre level. This is why there is such a demand for European-trained scientists in this country.[11]

In support of this, it is often pointed out that Americans themselves have been getting worried about school standards since the 1950s; and one of the Black Paper authors, Professor Richard Lynn, claims that similar results will follow should schools in Britain go comprehensive.[12]

As for the USSR, one line of approach is to argue that it has tried comprehensive education and found it wanting. In one version, the Russians have now turned away from it completely, have even developed 'the most highly selective system in the world',[13] have established special boarding schools for the élite;[14] in short, they have washed their hands of the whole Utopian notion. In less extreme versions, it has been pointed out that the system of unstreamed classes and uniform curricula involves a good deal of repetition, dull teaching, frustration and lack of initiative, and that the growth of special classes, and even of special schools for able children, is a natural reaction to this.

Robin Davis, a leading defender of selective schools, puts it thus:

The view that environment is all-important has had many adherents since Darwin, including the Marxists, who seem to 'favour
the conception of human beings emerging with perfect uniformity
from some conceptual conveyor-belt'; and it is becoming increasingly
fashionable, for obvious reasons, among those who favour comprehensive reorganisation, including the Minister himself. (This was written
during the term of the 1964–1970 Labour Government.) The Russians, on the other hand, or at any rate some Russian teachers, are
beginning to think there may be something in the concept of innate
ability after all. So we have the spectacle of a British Minister of
Education (sic) driving purposefully up a cul-de-sac and facing red-
faced Russian teachers moving tentatively in the opposite direction.
For this is a case where political and social wishful thinking flies
in the face of scientific evidence.[15]

Elsewhere, the same author mentions the development of accelerated courses as evidence of a Soviet change of heart. Leaving
aside the caricature of Marxist theory at the beginning of the
extract, and the sweeping assertion at the end, there is at least a
serious point here: in the Soviet Union, as in the USA, it has
been found the hard way that comprehensive education does not
work. The implications for Britain are clear enough; but the
same cannot be said for the evidence.

In the case of the USA, it is certainly true that the high
schools have unselective entry, and that the level of academic
attainment is, on the whole, lower than in English grammar
schools. Some caution has to be exercised, since one result of
having a decentralised system is that one finds more variation in
standards than, say, among the GCE examining boards. Nevertheless, most observers on both sides of the Atlantic are agreed
that in academic terms American high school graduates are well
behind English sixth-formers; and if the equation of American
seventeen-year-olds and English fifteen-year-olds is an oversimplification, it is not too wide of the mark. Many Americans
have been getting worried about this, notably since the launch-
ing of the first Soviet sputnik, and there have since then been
many calls from many quarters for the raising of standards and
greater rigour in the curriculum. The National Defense Education Act, which provides for federal aid for science teaching

programmes, has been one development from the disquiet over 'what Ivan knows that Johnny doesn't'.

But disquiet over mediocrity is one thing, rejection of comprehensive schooling is something else. In the first place, comprehensive education in America is generally taken to mean not only the provision of schooling for the entire neighbourhood in one secondary school, but 'something for everyone', with a wide range of elective and optional courses; among the multiplicity of course-offerings, three or four 'tracks' or course-types are generally provided, under such rubrics as 'college preparatory' (*i.e.* 'academic'), 'business and administration', 'technical and practical', etc. The fact that pupils attend the same school does not mean that they have to work at the same subjects at the same pace. Further, much of the school's attention is directed towards what in Britain might be regarded as non-scholastic matters – leisure activities, 'life-adjustment', social education and the like. The rationale behind this is complex, but it includes the assumption that the secondary school should cater for the total needs of the young adolescent, and that for *all* young people learning to live in their own society is a fundamental part of their education. Professor Dennis Brogan sums the position up thus:

If these millions of boys and girls are to be judged by their academic accomplishments they will be judged harshly. But they are not to be so judged, for their schools are doing far more than instruct them; they are letting them instruct each other in how to live in America.[16]

It may be thought, of course, that the attention given to non-scholastic activities is excessive, or that the emphasis on social education does not justify itself in practice. The second point is arguable, but this in any case does not invalidate the schools' objectives; and before making too much of the first, it is worth considering that the emphasis on games, 'character-building', 'leadership' and all the other imponderables of an English grammar or 'public' school may seem equally excessive to a Frenchman or a German. The academic superiority of the GCE 'A' level over the high school diploma is not in question, but unless we care to argue that only scholastic attainment counts, we must be prepared to accept the possibility that it has been gained at the expense of other objectives. Innumerable statements by grammar and 'public' school heads suggests that they are not, in fact, prepared to stand or fall by academic excellence alone.[17] Further, the much-vaunted 'A' level is rather less impressive when measured by the standards of the French *baccalauréat* or the German *Abitur*. By purely scholastic criteria, the grammar schools come further down in the international league than many care to believe; but if other criteria are admitted, then the social education of the American high schools cannot be dismissed quite so casually. The more exotic manifestations, such as cheer-leaders, dating rituals, flag-saluting ceremonies and the rest, doubtless look funny enough from the outside, but so do cricket and prefectorial installations and the assiduous cultivation of school traditions, real or more artificial. To single out one criterion for comparison is to prejudge, not advance, the argument.

Another serious flaw in this kind of argument is that it is not comparing like with like. Staying on at school is a normal expectation in America (hence the concern about those who do drop out); of the fourteen to seventeen age-group, over 94 per cent are in high school. The older ones may well lag in academic attainment behind the much smaller proportion finishing selective secondary courses in Britain, but to insist that they are behind those leaving secondary modern schools (as one would have to if consistent) is, to say the least, dubious. It may well be that this spread has been achieved at the expense of attainment among the abler twelfth-graders; but it must be remembered that half the age-group go on to some kind of higher education. Some of these enter two-year junior colleges, while others enter four-year colleges and drop out before finishing the course; all the same, over half the entrants finish some kind of degree course. It is true that standards at this level also vary considerably, and that they are often below European standards, but this is not the point. Even the worst colleges reach something like GCE standard, most of them considerably more (and, of course, many are quite as good as anything that Europe has to offer); and a much higher proportion of the age-group goes to college in the USA than enters grammar-school-type courses in England. This does mean that standards equivalent to 'A' level take longer to reach in America, but more get there in the end. If the process is slower, what is the fundamental objection? Nobody has managed to establish a mystical connection between age and optimum attainment in mathematics, say, or in history. Views of what it is reasonable to aim for at any level, whether primary, secondary or higher, have always been liable to change and are now changing faster than ever; witness, for example, the filtering into the secondary school of what was until recently university material in physics and chemistry, or the development of formerly secondary mathematics in the primary school. Taking high schools by themselves does not tell us enough; going to college is a standard expectation of a large proportion, almost a majority, of young Americans, and must therefore be taken into account.

It may be objected that America is a rich country, and can therefore afford to take its time, making up arrears at the tertiary stage, and similarly compensating for any lag in the colleges by the large-scale expansion of post-graduate courses. Britain, we are assured, cannot. As Lord James of Rusholme said after a visit to America some years ago:

A relatively poor country, dependent upon technical skill and maximum employment of ability for survival, must rely on an educational system that by selection and hard work and economical use of its teaching resources reaches a given level of attainment as early as possible. The clearest impression that one derives from the American educational scene is that the English grammar school is, quite simply, in our particular circumstances, one of our greatest hopes for our future national prosperity.[18]

It is of course perfectly true that if one is prepared to select a small enough group and concentrate teaching resources upon it, one can get it up to standards incomparably higher than the high school diploma or, for that matter, the GCE. Unfortunately such concepts as 'a given level of attainment' are not defined (given by whom?), the proportion is not specified, and 'as early as possible' could mean almost anything. No doubt it would be possible to bring a handful up to degree standard at fourteen, but this is not what those following the James line of argument seem to be suggesting. The Japanese have perfected techniques of training a few people up to almost superhuman heights of physical strength, at the cost of agility and proportion (they turn out to be enormously bulky, and find this, and their régime, an obstacle to normal social life); but the idea of producing a corps of intellectual Sumo wrestlers, though not impossible, has few advocates in Britain. A less extreme form of the argument would apply better to the German *Gymnasium*, which selects about 15 per cent of the age-group at *ten*, and provides a fiercely academic nine-year course leading to the *Abitur* certificate, which is about as far ahead of the GCE as the GCE is ahead of the high school diploma. This achievement is gained at a price: less than half the original intake actually pass the *Abitur* (the rest having failed or dropped out), while the average age of those who do finish is nearer twenty-one than nineteen – a system of such wastefulness that more and more Germans now accept it as a major cause of the 'German educational catastrophe'.[19] Significantly, plans for comprehensive re-organisation are under way in West Germany, and are meeting much less resistance than the far milder attempts at reform in the 1950s and early 1960s.[20]

But other doubts arise from the economic argument. Scotland is a 'relatively poor country' compared with England, yet admits a much higher proportion of the age-group to selective second-ary courses, aims for a standard lower, subject for subject, than the 'A' level (but requires a broader curriculum of subjects), and offsets this with a four-year instead of a three-year course for the honours degree – a system which, with all its faults, works tolerably well when not hacked about absent-mindedly by expatriate academics to conform to the quite different English system. This is a long way from the more leisurely American approach but, for all the obvious differences in atmosphere and tone, is much more like it than Lord James seems to think desirable or even possible in a country lacking American re-sources. If the more selective and accelerated English system does produce better results than the Scottish, this has yet to be demonstrated by something more convincing than assertion.

Now it is quite true that there is much soul-searching in America at present, but not quite in the terms suggested. Many feel that the schools and colleges are underachieving, that the pace is rather too leisurely, the courses too undemanding, the soft options too temptingly available. But this has not taken the form of a move towards selectivity, a solution favoured by so few American educationists that it is hardly an issue at all. Overwhelmingly, improvements are sought within the comprehensive framework; indeed, in many of the current controversies in American education – de facto segregation of neighbourhoods, the schools of the black ghettos, the use of counselling as a device for putting the poor and/or black into less ambitious courses, the growing trouble over finance in areas where more and more people live in one place and work in another – the burden of the complaint is that the schools are not comprehensive enough.[21]

Further, the 'America as a warning' approach is subject to another confusion, namely the assumption that because American schools are comprehensive, comprehensive schools must necessarily be like those in America. This is an assumption made by some of the Black Paper contributors (notably Professor Lynn), but it is no more logical than saying that because all mothers are women, all women must be mothers (and one does not have to be a Women's Lib militant to see the illogicality of that) or, to take an example offered in all seriousness by the South African government, that because Communists declare in favour of racial equality anyone who takes the same line must be a Communist.[22] For good or ill, the American high school is not only comprehensive but American, and is therefore liable to reflect the values, preoccupations and problems of American society. Just how different a comprehensive system can be is demonstrated by the other favourite illustration of the selection lobby, the USSR.

The Soviet school, like the American, is based in the last analysis on an egalitarian philosophy, but the practical interpretations are poles apart. To say that the American school fits the curriculum to the pupil and the Soviet school the pupil to the curriculum is an oversimplification, but there is something in it. The Soviet school tends to assume that any pupil, unless he is clinically subnormal, lazy or badly taught, can make something of an 'academically respectable' course. Consequently, all Soviet children follow much the same syllabus at much the same pace, generally in unstreamed mixed-ability classes.

Standards are always difficult to compare; even within the British Isles, there is still no satisfactory way of comparing groups of passes in the GCE and the Scottish counterpart, for instance. One still has to make use of impressions: at the end of the eighth form of the Soviet general school (age fifteen), the work being done is not unlike that of the middle range of grammar-school children of the same age. At the end of the tenth class, the work being done for the *attestat zrelosti* (certificate of maturity) does not measure up to GCE 'A' level in any one subject, but it can be reasonably compared with a Scottish 'group' which, like the Soviet certificate, is based on the principle of carrying forward a wider range of subjects each to a more modest level. There are other difficulties in making comparisons: the Soviet system covers a somewhat wider range, and does not distinguish between levels or grades ('O' and 'H' or 'O' and 'A'); but it does seem that the Soviet syllabus works on the principle that practically all children can cope with work that in Britain is thought to come within the compass of only the top third or so. Some reservations have to be made: most of the assessment is oral and much attention is given to classwork, which leaves room for leniency. Children who do not make the grade have to repeat the year's work, and although the proportion doing this has been decreasing (almost to vanishing-point in the cities, it is claimed) it is still substantial in the countryside (where half the population lives).[23] But when all due allowances have been made, it does appear that the depression of standards so gleefully pointed out in the American high schools is not general in the comprehensive schools in the USSR.

There are still plenty of problems, of course. Few Soviet teachers deny that mixed-ability groups can raise problems. Experiments (albeit cautious) are being made with 'setting'; there has been some move away from the uniform curriculum, which was criticised as leaving too little room for the development of the pupils' individual interests; there are indications that not enough has been done to stretch the abler pupils; and in some areas, mainly rural, there have been complaints of apathy;[24] and since much of the success of the uniform curriculum has depended on sheer hard slog, the price of frequently dull or dogmatic teaching has to be paid.

These and other problems have been conspicuously aired in the last few years and a number of changes have been made. One goes back to the late 1950s. While overhauling the whole educational system, Khrushchev suggested extending the principle of special schools (there were already long-established ten-year schools for music, art, ballet and the like) to mathematics and the natural sciences. This gave rise to some press controversy, and little more was heard of the idea. Later, a modified version made its appearance; there are now a few upper secondary schools (taking children at fifteen plus) for the winners of national competitions in physics and mathematics.[25]

Another and more recent development has been the growth of optional and elective courses. These came in with the Khrushchev reforms in 1958 in a very small way – one hour a week in the final year. The time for options has been growing ever since, and now amounts to two hours a week in the seventh and eighth forms, six in the ninth and tenth. The object is to enable pupils to study further something already on the curriculum, or to add something different. The idea of 'enrichment' is not, of course, new; this has long been available in school 'circles' (spare-time interest-groups or clubs) and the Pioneer Palaces and Houses, run by the youth organisations. The introduction of options was hardly radical, but rather the formalisation of this kind of variety within the official curriculum as well. In the many articles[26] dealing with these courses, phrases like 'individual interests', 'personal initiative', and the like occur with a frequency surprising to anyone more used to the 'perfect uniformity' and 'conveyor-belt' imagery used by Mr Davis.

Now it is quite true that devices of this kind can develop into something not unlike 'setting', a moderate concession to the principles both of specialisation and differentiated instruction. Indeed, many Eastern European countries have taken 'special classes' and 'accelerated language groups' rather further.[27] There are also indications that many Soviet teachers do divide classes into fast and slow groups in any case, whether approved or not. But to describe this as a retreat from comprehensive schooling is accurate only if one assumes that differentiation has no place within the comprehensive school. It is certainly a move away from completely uniform courses, but that is only one type of comprehensive organisation; nor is the alternative necessarily a system of rigid streaming.

To insist that the growing recognition of individual differences must be a denial of the comprehensive principle rests on the assumption that the Soviet schools are comprehensive because they do not recognise any difference in ability. But this is a caricature of the position. Marxists certainly emphasise environmental rather than hereditary factors, and view the concept of inherited intelligence rather warily. But this does not mean that they deny the very existence of innate ability (though some of the more dogmatic formulations do sometimes give this impression). As the opening sentence of a recent Soviet book on the subject says, 'Children's aptitudes vary considerably; Marxist science does not deny the existence of these differences', and the author goes on to stress the importance of upbringing in realising children's potential.[28] What they do reject is the biologically deterministic approach; they prefer to concentrate on what *can* be affected by education rather than what cannot. It can be argued that insisting on a uniform curriculum for all was going too far, though results have been better than believers in a fixed 'pool of ability' could have expected. The provision of more flexible courses, within the comprehensive framework, has been developing for over a decade, and is still continuing. But to describe this as 'red-faced Russian teachers moving tentatively in the opposite direction' is to confuse the issue. No 'British Minister of Education'[29] has ever advocated uniform curricula; once again, it must be stressed that there is more than one kind of comprehensive education.

The special schools are a different matter. They are selective and are thus obvious exceptions to the comprehensive pattern. One must, however, distinguish between the art schools, which generally offer all-through ten-year courses, and the handful of science schools, which admit pupils from the eighth form. Two further reservations have to be made about both types. Firstly, they cater for *special* talents, not for clever children generally; their role is thus more like that of the Yehudi Menuhin School than Manchester Grammar or Winchester. Secondly, the numbers involved are very small. On both counts, the creaming-off effect is negligible; they do not constitute a category of schools for the able at the expense of the rest.

It would be naïve to suppose that the USSR has yet achieved equality in education; as the Soviet Press makes abundantly clear, there are still educational haves and have-nots. But the main gap is not between working-class and professional-class children, but between town and country. In the rural areas there are still more small schools, the teacher supply problem is much more acute, distance adds to the problems of communication and supply, and centrally-determined standards are harder to implement. The picture is uneven, but there can be little doubt that the level of attainment is lower than in the towns, and there is still considerable 'leakage' from the schools before the official leaving-age.[30] Attempts are being made to improve the position by providing more boarding schools, though not so far on an effective scale (boarding schools are extremely expensive to provide, a place costing over seven times as much as one in a day school),[31] and the universities are now organising special preparatory courses to enable students from rural schools to catch up with their urban counterparts.[32] The main difficulty is that living standards are lower in the country than in the town, amenities are scarcer, and teachers are reluctant to go there – in spite of free housing, the abolition of pay differentials that used to favour the urban teacher, and (doubtfully effective) powers of direction for up to three years. While these inequalities remain, so will the problem; but it is hard to see what this has to do with comprehensive schooling as such.

In a very real sense, in fact, the Soviet system is becoming *more* comprehensive. The 1958 'Khrushchev reforms' established an eight-year school from seven to fifteen, followed by a tripartite structure of general secondary school, specialised secondary school (with professional orientation), or a less demanding trade school. Pupils could leave at fifteen, though the option of taking part-time secondary courses was still open. At the time, work-based or part-time courses were officially preferred. Only a minority went on with full-time general schooling, and it seemed likely to many observers that as soon as the effects of the last-war population gap had worn off, the demand for places would bring in some kind of selection at the fifteen-plus stage.

This has not happened. The demand for places has risen, but the number of places has risen faster. About 60 per cent of the age-group are now attending the senior classes, and there are complaints from the Ministry that this is still not enough. The problem, after all, is not one of selectivity but unfulfilled targets.[33] Present policy is to make some kind of complete secondary schooling compulsory in the near future (the earlier target-date of 1970–71 having proved rather optimistic, at any rate in the countryside); and it is now held that the most desirable way of doing this is to complete the general secondary full-time school, though a minority will still be able to take the more professional courses. There are still a great many practical problems, but the intention is clearly to make general secondary schooling the normal experience of Soviet youngsters, with increased flexibility within a comprehensive system.[34] This can hardly be described as a retreat from comprehensive education by Soviet teachers, red-faced or otherwise.

What, then, has the experience of other countries operating comprehensive systems to offer? First of all, it makes it clear that there are many models for such a system, and provides warnings against drawing facile conclusions from American scholastic standards or Soviet rigidity. Secondly, it shows that although there are reappraisals leading to many changes, these are taking place within the comprehensive framework. To insist that it shows that comprehensive education does not work is to misuse the evidence.

It also demonstrates that some problems are *not* solved by comprehensive reorganisation. Some, such as the increase in private schooling in America and Sweden, or the correlation of class with area (slums and suburbia in the USA, town and country in the USSR) are, if anything, highlighted. But such problems spread far beyond the school, and so must the solutions. Selectivity does not so much solve the problems as sweep them under the carpet.

Another issue in which the experience of other nations is pressed into service is the expansion of higher education. The attack is two-pronged, offering nightmares of overcrowding, alienation and probably chaos on the one hand, and an inevitable decline of standards on the other. France is much cited, especially since the *évènements* of 1968; so is America, with the spread of campus disorders from California to Columbia, culminating in the riots at Kent State, Ohio, in 1970, during which four students were shot dead. Apart from actual disturbances, the increase of size consequent upon expansion of higher education is said to turn the universities into vast, impersonal degree-factories, where students are processed through courses of a generally low standard. Undergraduate courses that would not tax an English sixth-former, and B.A.s in football and

Ph.D.s in driving or cosmetics are firmly fixed in the European mind as typical of the American scene, thus enabling everyone to feel superior to the Americans and at the same time demonstrate that 'more means worse'. For good measure, the French and American drop-out rates are contrasted with our own. Once again, the implications are obvious: the experience of others in attempting to move away from the idea of higher education limited to an élite is fraught with danger, producing at worst upheaval and at best depersonalised mediocrity. Our own time-tested ways, by contrast, appear much safer.

That the universities of France and the United States, among others, have been the scene of major and violent disturbances is beyond question, and it would be foolish to try to shrug them off. There is little agreement, however, about the causes, but ample ground for thinking that to put them all down to expansion alone, or even mainly, is altogether too simple.

Let us consider France first. It is quite true that many French universities had, in the expansion of recent years, become extremely large. They had, on average, about 19,000 students at the time of the 1968 disturbances, much more in the Sorbonne. Further, in spite of attempts to take off some of the pressure by opening new complexes (like Nanterre), facilities were still desperately short, since they had not expanded at the same rate or anything like it. There were, of course, other factors behind the explosion, among them graduate unemployment, bad relations with the authorities, growing impatience with a sclerotic system, a wider malaise in French society (the students were, after all, only one category of dissidents) and, as a trigger, the brutal behaviour of the police in breaking up a demonstration which, as usual, had the effect of making things worse. Still, it may be claimed that overcrowding and lack of tuition and facilities was one element in the situation.

But this does not mean that expansion was the cause in itself. In the first place, expansion need not mean pouring quarts into pint pots. Where this happens, there is of course likely to be trouble (as also in Italy, for example), but this is the fault of unintelligent planning. Secondly, the expansion was not, in fact, great by British, let alone American, standards; the proportion going on to higher education is smaller in France than in Britain (once again, this is true also of Italy). Thirdly, the trouble has not been confined to big or overcrowded universities. Since 1968, in particular, unrest has spread in two directions: downwards into the *lycées* (the counterpart, roughly, of the grammar schools), and upwards into the *grandes écoles*, the élite professional schools. Of these, the *École Normale Supérieure* (Higher Teachers' School, where the upper echelons of the teaching profession are trained) recently closed down, and its rector resigned, after riots. In this case, numbers can hardly be blamed; the ENS, like other *grandes écoles*, caters for a tiny élite, admitting some forty students a year out of ten times that number of applicants. Nor can this be a question of more meaning worse; although the universities have admitted virtually every applicant with the *baccalauréat* or school leaving certificate (in itself a qualification of high standard), the *grandes écoles* require two years of further study *after* the *baccalauréat*, and teach at a level well above that of the universities, themselves quite as good as anything in Britain. Yet they have had trouble too;[35] and just in case there is any temptation to attribute events to 'lax discipline' in the universities, it may be worth mentioning that the regime in the *grandes écoles* is near-military. The pat answers (and the extrapolations from them to our own situation) will not do.

Incidentally, it is quite true that the rate of drop-out from French universities has, by British standards, been startlingly high – up to 70 per cent in the late 1960s (compared with about two per cent from the *grandes écoles*).[36] But before this is taken as a vindication of the 'more means worse' line, it must be remembered that in the French system it is difficult to know who are the 'real' students; since anyone with the *bac* can enter, many do so because they find it cheap or congenial to use student facilities while doing something else altogether. Further, the first degree (*license*) is gained by collecting a number of course-credits or *certificats*, rather like the American, Scottish or Open University system; many employers recognise one or two *certificats* as qualifications in their own right, without insisting on completion of the degree. Once again, it is not known how many enrol for this purpose; in all probability, few have the definite intention of doing this when they first go to university, but the fact that many do must be borne in mind when considering drop-out. Even in terms of paper qualifications, the time of these people has not been wasted. And it is still not universally assumed that qualification must always be the purpose of going to university – a fairly recent notion, as we have seen, in Britain as well. It may nevertheless worry the authorities that so many do not finish, for whatever reason; but this does not necessarily mean that the French student body is mediocre, or has declined through casting the net more widely in the national pool of ability.

What, then, of the United States, where there *is* a mass higher education system, and where this is held to have been achieved at the cost of the huge 'multiversities', where restless and overcrowded students are processed through mediocre courses?

First of all, it would be as well to get a few facts straight.[37] Many American universities *are* enormous. There are 261,000 students in the State University of New York, for example. Most of the very biggest are multi-campus universities, such as California, Texas, Wisconsin or Missouri, and it may be more realistic to consider their component colleges; even so, one is still struck by the hugeness of many of the better-known – Berkeley, California, has 25,000 students, and many single campuses are even bigger, like Ohio State (Columbus), with 35,000. Perhaps it is not surprising that most people, Americans as well as foreigners, tend to think of the typical American university as a massive institution with tens or even hundreds of thousands of teeming students.

Common they may be, but they are not typical. It is all too easy to forget the enormous range, from New York State or Penn State to the Mennonite Biblical Seminary, Elkhart (Ind.), with forty-five students and a teaching faculty of seven. Even within the single state of Ohio, for example, there are twenty-two universities ranging from Ohio State to Wilberforce (Xenia) with under a thousand students. It is easy to overlook, also, the numbers involved. According to the US Office of Education, there are over 2,400 higher educational institutions in the country (to be precise, 1,472 private, 1,011 public, with 2,036,000 and 4,892,000 students respectively).[38] Since there is nothing to stop anyone from opening a university and awarding degrees, there may be some doubt about how many of these institutions can be considered 'real' universities, and many protect themselves by submitting to inspection by accrediting agencies which give, as it were, a certificate of academic respectability. Now, if we count only senior accredited colleges (that is, leaving out all two-year junior colleges, together with any senior colleges *not* recognised, like Ian Paisley's *alma mater* Bob Jones), we can reduce the 2,400-odd institutions to some 1,100. Of these, many do come into the giant category – nearly 5 per cent have over 20,000, 12 per cent over 10,000. But the majority are much smaller than Edinburgh or Oxford, not to mention London or Lyon or Heidelberg: three-quarters have fewer than 5,000 students, over half have fewer than 2,000, 30 per cent have under 1,000. The average is around 4,500. Nor is there much connection between size and 'quality', however determined, either way. True, Berkeley has 25,000 and Columbia 17,000, but then Kent State has 27,000, and is not exactly at the top of the pecking order. Contrariwise, Vassar has 1,600, Princeton around 4,000, while many other 'prestige schools', public and private, have between 5,000 and 8,000. M.I.T., for instance, has just over 7,000 students. There are, then, good and poor big universities, good and poor small ones, and practically every combination that one can conceive. Prominent though the giants are, they play a less important part than is usually thought in the mass provision of higher education in the United States; this can be more reasonably attributed to the proliferation of small and medium-sized colleges.

Faced with the range of American higher institutions, and a common career structure, it might be useful in the present discussion to determine what proportions of young Americans go to 'real' universities. The accrediting system does not really help a great deal; the standards required are far from exacting, and include the 'Ivy League' and major state institutions in the same category as Corpus Christi University, Texas (student population, 550), which advertises 'Sun, surf and sand' as its main attractions. Whether one is trying to demonstrate the awfulness of most American higher education, or to show that the majority do in fact go to 'good schools', is by the way; the exercise, so far, has proved quite futile. Subjectivity, and the extent of intra- as well as inter-college variation, see to that. Further, most higher institutions see the provision of broad general courses as part of their function. Many of these could be reasonably compared with an English sixth-form or French *lycée* or German *Gymnasium* course, for reasons that we have seen already; but this does not necessarily affect the standing of the university or college itself. As a rule, what gives a university prestige is what happens at the other end of the process – that is, effective graduate and professional schools. With the burgeoning of graduate schools in what used to be simply four-year colleges, this too is becoming more difficult to assess. One is always hearing of Ph.D.s in driver education or sport, and it is common knowledge that there are some universities whose higher degrees are at least as good as anything taken in Europe. The extremes are easy enough to distinguish; the difficulty, as usual, is knowing where to draw the line in between.

Even the quality of teaching faculty (however one determines *that*) is not always a reliable guide to the standing of an institution. Once again, there are some about whose standing there is no dispute. But many relatively mediocre universities have found that money can be well spent in establishing a number of special appointments, suitably garnished with high salaries and research grants, which will tempt a few 'big names' to come, at least for a while, and thus raise the general level, or at least the reputation.

The American colleges, then, whether large or small, public or private, embrace such a variety that almost any generalisation becomes hazardous. Just how many of them can be reckoned as good, bad or indifferent is largely a matter of opinion; there is certainly no objective criterion that will stand up. *Some* are enormous; *some* have modest standards of attainment; *some* fill the functions of European secondary schools. But it has yet to be demonstrated that any of these qualities coincide, or that any are necessary consequences of expansion. Incidentally, the other obvious example of massive expansion of higher education is in the Soviet Union; and although there are problems there too, and though many criticisms can be and are made (such as rigidity), dilution of academic standards is not one of them. Nor has it produced student unrest on any appreciable scale. The absence of this can, of course, be attributed to other factors in Soviet society at large, which might well be thought undesirable; but the converse equally applies to the *presence* of unrest in the United States.

As for student participation, there is little evidence that this has much to do with unrest either. The extent to which students are involved with the running of their institutions varies a great deal, from full participation to none; so far, no correlation has been demonstrated at any university between the degree of involvement and the incidence of trouble.

In Latin America, the position is rather different. The universities there are, generally, independent of governmental control (unlike the state universities in America), and one does often find in many of them student control associated with political infighting, disturbances and other phenomena of that kind. Now it is possible to argue that student participation in university government is 'utterly nonsensical', as Mr Enoch Powell has put it.[39] If the reasoning is less than clear, it is still a point of view. But he offers the Latin American scene as an example of what is likely to stem from it, and this prospect is certainly likely to frighten most academics, voters and probably many students as well. But Britain is not Latin America; in most countries on that continent, the scope for political debate or action is or has been limited in the extreme. The universities have managed to survive as autonomous units free of the restraints that affect most other areas of national life and thus fill, in an exaggerated hothouse form, the functions which in Britain are filled by Parliament, the press, television, open-air meetings and the like. The two situations are hardly comparable. In Britain the pressure on the universities to become a focus of political activity is slight; in many Latin American countries it is overwhelming, since there is no alternative. (Some might like to add that there is also more to complain *about*, though of course this is a subjective judgement, not a fact.)

When we pass on to the dire outcome of 'progressive' education, a major difficulty arises immediately. 'Progressive' education, like that other popular conceptual rag-bag, 'permissiveness', is at best a pretty vague term; it is far more effective as a hooray-word or boo-word, according to taste, than a description of any coherent philosophy. In the 1920s there was, or seemed to be, a fairly identifiable progressive movement, working on the assumption that children were (1) human, (2) individuals rather than members of a class and (3) people in their own right and not merely future adults; that learning was both more effective and more enjoyable if combined with practical activity and/or play, and that coercion and punishment were not a good basis for teacher–pupil relations or the educational process. It took a variety of forms, many based on American experiences, including the 'play-way', the Dalton Plan (which based most of children's learning on individual work-assignments rather than formal class-teaching), the project method (where things were learned through the group solution of some task on which they had a bearing), and so on. There were also a number of more specifically anti-authoritarian ventures, based on the idea of complete freedom for children within a self-governing community. These are generally associated with particular individuals; Homer Lane's Little Commonwealth, and A. S. Neill's Summerhill (still going strong) are probably the best known, but there are others.[40] In popular parlance, the label 'progressive' is attached (for praise or blame) to many other unconnected developments – look and say reading, colour-coded reading, the initial teaching alphabet, Cuisenaire arithmetic, the new mathematics, free composition, anything at all out of the way in art, music or drama teaching, sex education (of course), and practically anything else introduced since the turn of the century. All that these have in common is a suspicion of rote learning and (sometimes) authoritarianism. Few of them are particularly new; Dewey was advocating project methods early in the present century; Pestalozzi was trying out his ideas of practical learning during the Napoleonic wars; Rousseau was airing his seminal ideas (such as the importance of play, the training of the senses, learning by doing, etc.) before the French Revolution, and some of *his* ideas were being advocated (and to some extent practised) by Comenius and his contemporaries in the seventeenth century.[41] It is quite misleading to talk of 'progressivism' as if it were either a new or structured school of thought. Most primary school teachers have been making extensive use of 'progressive' techniques for generations, but it is unlikely that many of them would understand much of the philosophy of Rousseau or Dewey or sympathise much with that of Neill or Aikenhead.

Now it is broadly true that some of the progressive *methods* are more widely used in the United States than in Europe; and it is also true that standards are generally lower and violence much more common. But to argue cause and effect from this, as many try to do, is to make several unwarranted assumptions. To begin with, not all American schools are 'progressive'; many are bleak, formal and authoritarian. Since these are more likely to be found in urban ghettoes than elsewhere, and since that is where the standards are lowest and the violence most rampant, it might be tempting to argue that these are caused by *non*-progressive teaching.[42] But this will not do either, for it is arguing correlations to causes, always a risky procedure – especially when we lack sufficient evidence about the effective extent of 'progressivism' in America at the present time. In any case, we have seen that the whole question of school standards is far from simple, and violence in America is far too widespread and deep a problem to attach to any one cause. There are many, and the type of classroom regime is perhaps the least likely to be decisive when one considers race, housing, unemployment, international crises and the other headaches that American society as a whole (not just its schools) is beset with at the moment.

As for Scandinavia, the conclusions one draws rather depend on our view of the prevailing *mores*. Some critics,[43] notably Mr David Holbrook, see something immensely sinister in what they hold to be the Scandinavian obsession with sex; Denmark's abolition of censorship is made much of in this respect. It is, of course, a matter of taste whether one sees anything wrong with a franker approach; it does not necessarily prove that this makes their actual behaviour much different from our own, or that it would be particularly reprehensible if it did. These are value-judgements, not facts. But if the issue is to be confused by going on about 'pornography for children' (in which Mr David Holbrook sees close parallels with Nazi Germany), it may be worth stressing one or two points. For one thing, Scandinavia is not uniform; in Sweden, the law with regard to pornography and minors is similar to that in Britain. Only in Denmark has control been totally abolished; and all the indications are that the incidence of sex-crimes, *and* the demand for pornography (at least among Danes) has gone down.[44] Even if one does care to equate frankness about and interest in sex with moral degeneracy – a not uncommon view in Britain – there is not much to connect it with the regime or organisation of the schools. (If we are dragging the Nazis in, and thus ignoring the totally different

attitudes in Scandinavia and pre-war Germany towards practically everything, including race, violence and war as well as
sex, it may be worth remembering that the society that produced the bizarre activities of 1930s Berlin had one of the most
authoritarian school systems in Europe.)[45] Incidentally, if we
can drag the discussion away from sex for a moment, nobody
seems to have tried to prove that 'progressive' education had
produced lower scholastic standards in Scandinavia; it would,
of course, be difficult.

The trouble with so many of these excursions into foreign
parts in search of evidence is that they end up in mythical
systems, not the real ones; and even when some of the facts are
accurate, they are distorted through being wrenched from context and strained through a stereotypical sieve. The American
system, for instance, is depicted as fanatically levelling, raw and
inexperienced, lacking in tradition, breaking up in confusion
and radicalism, thus warning against disturbing stable systems
with well-tried values. Alternatively, it is high-powered, original, informal, up-to-date, efficient, uninhibited and bubbling
over with creative energy and ideas.

The truth lies nearer the opposite of these assertions, favourable or unfavourable. The schools are far less levelling than they
appear; most of them are unsegregated neighbourhood schools,
to be sure, but at least in the larger towns the neighbourhoods
are segregated by race, class or both.[46] Higher education is no
longer the preserve of an élite, but it contains élite preserves.
Though Americans are prone to make much of the newness of
their system, the pedigree goes far back.[47] Many of the New
England colonies had effective school systems in the eighteenth
century, when in Europe this could be said only of Prussia, the
Netherlands, Scotland and probably some Swiss cantons and
one or two of the German states, like Baden-Württemberg. Indeed, the Massachusetts School Law, which provided not only
for elementary schools but secondary schools as well, was passed
in 1647. Similarly with the universities: Harvard was founded
in 1637, William and Mary in 1693, Yale in 1701, Dartmouth in
1769, Columbia in 1754 and the State Universities of Georgia
and North Carolina in 1785 and 1789 respectively – all at a time
when England had two universities and Scotland four. Whether
the lack of a continuous educational tradition is a crippling

disadvantage is a matter of opinion; if it is, the Americans should be the last to worry, for in many ways it is more genuine than our own (Britain having borrowed extensively from America during the nineteenth and twentieth centuries). There are complementary myths here, America's myth of its newness and Britain's of its antiquity. These appear to be the ways we like to think of ourselves on our respective sides of the Atlantic, but they are far less true than either of us usually supposes. Indeed, there is a case to be made for the view that American education is, at bottom, hidebound by tradition, thus inhibiting both efficiency and originality, creativity or informality, in all of which the semblance is much easier to realise than the substance.

The Soviet system is seen as rigidly uniform, insisting that everyone must be the same, forcing everyone into the same mould. The curriculum is narrowly specialised, suffused with science, and the humanities have only a small part to play. The schools are grim institutions, impersonal, joyless, harshly disciplined and in some versions are anti-family as well. On the other hand, it is allowed that at least they are efficient in a rather machine-like way, tightly planned, carefully organised, and quite uninhibited with anything so sentimental as an attachment to the past.

Again, most of these characteristics take on a rather different look under closer scrutiny. We have already seen how shaky some of the assertions about uniformity are. As for specialisation, it is necessary to distinguish the various stages of the educational process. In the general school, even with the introduction of the optional element, the curriculum is a good deal *less* specialised than in an English secondary school; *all* pupils study Russian language, literature, history, geography, nature study, social studies, biology, physics, chemistry, mathematics, technical drawing, work study, a foreign language, physical education, art, music and in the case of older pupils, astronomy. Very roughly, the curricular time breaks down, in classes IV–X, thus: science 37 per cent, humanities 40 per cent, other subjects 10 per cent, options 13 per cent.[48] Senior pupils can use the time for options to increase the proportion of science to half of the total time, or of humanities to just over half. This is much less specialised than the curriculum of grammar-school pupils.

At university or college level, it is true that the main area of
study has to be selected from the beginning of the course (like
England, but unlike Scotland); all the same, a 'specialism'
covers a wide range of components, and the time for options
and for compulsory general elements (PE, foreign language,
educational and socio-political courses) can be as high as a third
of the total. Again, it is true that science looms large in the
curricula of the general schools, but so do the arts; and although much has been said about the 'polytechnisation' of education (requiring all pupils to study the principles and practice
of industrial production), there is another side to the coin,
namely the humanisation of technology – students in trade
schools, for instance, are required to continue with a substantial
element of non-technical material. Judging both from official
statements and what happens in the schools, 'many-sided' education is still taken very seriously in the Soviet Union. The
school regime is certainly formal, even old-fashioned, but not as
grim as is often made out. Some teachers *are* unimaginative and
impersonal, some are martinets; but a great many are neither
and, for what it is worth, teacher training programmes make a
great deal of the importance of friendly relations between
teachers and pupils. If many, inevitably, fall short on this score,
it is a matter for comment and reproof. Discipline is certainly
fairly tight by the standards of *some* British schools, but although there is a battery of penalties available to the teacher at
need, ranging from a mild reproof up to a severe reprimand or
even a lowering of the conduct mark, physical punishment is
not one of them. As for the family, it is true that in the early
post-revolutionary days there were attempts to weaken its ties;
present policy, however, is almost obsessional about the need to
involve families, and there is an elaborate system of parents'
committes, home visiting, parents' conferences and so forth to
ensure this. In boarding schools, the view taken is that parental
involvement becomes more, not less, important.[49]

The positive features are overdrawn too. There is plenty of
central planning of the most detailed kind, right down to the
content of the school syllabus, teaching methods and the like. It
is, however, much less efficient than is sometimes claimed; one
of the commonest complaints in the Soviet press is that decisions taken at the centre have not been properly implemented

in practice, or that planning has come unstuck. The failure to ensure educational equality in the countryside is the most serious outcome of this, but there are many other cases.[50] As for the willingness to break with the past and carry out bold innovations, this is often more apparent than real. Educational conservatism can be a strong influence still; in fact, it is often the rock on which centrally determined reforms (especially in teaching methods) can founder in practice. For good or ill, there is more flexibility in the system than an examination of the official mechanisms would suggest.

There are not quite so many myths of a general nature about the systems of other countries, mainly because little notice has been taken of them except in times of major crisis (as in France, for example). There are a few. In Germany, for instance, the stereotype of the drill-sergeant of a Prussian schoolmaster has more or less disappeared, and if there is a general picture of the German system it is more likely to be one of cool efficiency and modernisation, befitting the land of the present-day *Wirtschaftswunder* and the powerful Deutschmark. Alas for neatness, the West German system is, structurally at least, one of the most old-fashioned and backward-looking in Europe (in Northern Europe, anyway), nor is it particularly efficient, if the enormous drop-out rate from secondary schools is anything to go by; and reforms which all parties accepted quite cheerfully in England in 1945 were still being condemned as destructive, subversive and Marxist by powerful sections of German opinion when attempts were being made to introduce them, tentatively, in the 1950s and 1960s.[51]

None of this means that evidence from other systems cannot be used to help understand our own, but it has to be accurate, not mythological. Even when the facts *are* correct, they have to be examined in context; otherwise, it is easy to miss the point that difficulties of, say, comprehensive schooling are connected with many factors in the society as a whole, which may well be quite irrelevant to our own case. Also, parts of an educational system have to be looked at in the context of the whole – a secondary school in a system where half go on to college is not the same kind of thing as one which marks the end of formal education for the bulk of its pupils. Most important of all, perhaps, is the need to take account of educational objectives; as we have seen in the case of the USA, it is not very sensible to jump to the conclusion that a system is failing without trying to find out what it is trying to do in the first place. If we insist on judging by our own criteria, we are loading the argument in advance – which may be comforting, but it is a comfort based on a delusion.

Unless these factors are taken into account, and unless we can make the leap in the imagination to realise that our own values may not be self-evidently right and good to all mankind, we are not really gaining from international experience, but merely misunderstanding the systems of other countries as a way of further misunderstanding our own.

REFERENCES

1. 'The Bestiary' (B. M. Arundel 292). In: Joseph Hall. *Selections from Early Middle English* (Oxford, 1920), XXI, pp. 176–86.

2. St Augustine said that wild animals existed to punish men, to test them, to exercise them, or to instruct them. (St Augustine, *Omnia Opera*, Gaume, Paris, 1836). Vol. iii, Pt. I, p. 259. Similarly, Topsell's *Historie of Foure-footed Beastes* (1607) was intended to lead men to 'heavenly meditation upon earthly creatures'. These and other examples may be found in Bergen Evans, *The Natural History of Nonsense* (Michael Joseph, 1947).

3. Ernest Seton Thompson, *The Natural History of the Ten Commandments* (New York, 1907).

4. Konrad Lorenz, *King Solomon's Ring* (Methuen, 1952). Lorenz also questions the legendary savagery of wolves.

5. Van Lawick-Goodall, *The Gentle Killers* (1971). Field observations showed that the widely-assumed roles of lion and hyena are frequently reversed.

6. Robert Ardrey, *African Genesis* (Collins, 1961).

7. Sally Carrighar, *Wild Heritage* (Panther, 1967), p. 131.

8. Robert Graves represents Livy as saying: 'Any legendary episode from early historical writings which bears on my theme of the ancient greatness of Rome I gladly incorporate in the story: though it may not be true in factual detail, it is true in spirit. If I come across two versions of the same episode I choose the one nearest to my theme . . .' (Graves, *I, Claudius*, Penguin, 1953, p. 109.) This is, of course, a fictional account, but it merely makes a little more explicit the statements of intent in Livy's own writing.

9. Poll by Opinion Research Centre, *Sunday Times*, 27 May 1973.

10. Many of these assertions may be found in various places in the *Black Papers* (*loc. cit.*), in Robin Davis, *The Grammar School* (Penguin, 1967), etc.

11. Quoted in Robin Davis, *op. cit.*, p. 145.

12. Professor Richard Lynn of Dublin.

13. This was stated during a Commons debate on comprehensive schooling, and apparently passed unchallenged.

14. Mr Harold Macmillan, in a speech arguing the inevitability and rightness of selective schooling, described Soviet boarding schools as 'Muscovite Etons'.

15. Davis, *op. cit.*, p. 172.

16. Dennis Brogan, *The American Character* (New York, 1944).

17. See, for example, Frances Stevens, *The Living Tradition.* Some of the statements from this and other sources are given in Brian Jackson and Dennis Marsden, *Education and the Working Class* (Penguin, 1966), pp. 237 ff.

18. *Times Educational Supplement*, November, 1957, quoted in Davis, *op. cit.*, p. 189.

19. Georg Picht, *Die deutsche Bildungskatastrophe* (Walter-Verlag, 1964).

20. For earlier reactions, see Saul B. Robinsohn and J. Caspar Kuhlmann, 'Two decades of non-reform in West German education', *Comparative Education Review* (October 1967), XI, 3, pp. 311–30.

21. 'Bussing' of students from one area to another, the cause of much heated controversy in American politics, is essentially an attempt to redress the social (and racial) balance in situations where neighbourhoods, rather than schools, have become selective.

22. The classic example is the Suppression of Communism Act.

23. *Finansy SSSR*, 10. 1966, pp. 10–11, gives the rural repeating rate as one and a half times that of the towns. It may well be higher. For some of the social implications of the town/country disparities, see Murray Yanowitch and Norton Dodge, 'Social class and education: some Soviet findings and reactions'. *Comparative Education Review* (October 1968), XII, 3, pp. 248–67.

24. V. Zalivadnyi, 'Na puti iz vos'mogo v devyatyi'. *Uchitel'skaya gazeta*, 11 April 1967.

25. N. Grant, *Soviet Education* (Penguin, 1972).

26. *E.g.* Akademiya pedagogicheskikh nauk RSFSR, *Obshchaya ob'yasnitel'naya zapiska k pererabotannym proektam uchebnogo plana i programm srednei shkoly* (Moscow, 1965).

27. N. Grant, *Society, Schools and Progress in Eastern Europe* (Pergamon, 1969).

28. G. S. Prozorov, *Heredity and Upbringing* (Moscow, 1960), p. 3.

29. It may be a small point, but there is not and never has been a 'British Minister of Education'; the Secretary of State for Education and Science (like the Minister of former times) is responsible for the school system of England and Wales only.

30. A. Zaitsev, 'Vazhnaya zadacha'. *Narodnoe obrazovanie* 8, 1966. p. 9.

31. Harold Noah, *Financing Soviet Schools* (Columbia, 1966), pp. 109 ff.

32. *Komsomol'skaya pravda*, 11 March 1969; *Pravda*, 6 September 1969; *Pravda*, 23 October 1969.

33. M. A. Prokofiev, 'K novomu pod'emu sovetskoi shkoly.' *Uchitel'skaya gazeta*, 26 November 1966.

34. V TsK KPSS i Sovete Ministrov SSSR: O merakh dal'neishemu uluchsheniyu raboty srednei obshcheobrazovatel'noi shkoly. *Pravda*, 19 November 1966, and Prokofiev, *loc. cit.*

35. Brian Holmes, *New Academic*, 1, 6 May 1971. For an account and analysis of the 1968 disturbances, see Charles Posner (Ed.), *Reflections on the Revolution in France: 1968* (Penguin, 1970).

36. W. D. Halls, *Society, Schools and Progress in France* (Pergamon, 1965), Ch. 9. This was written before recent changes in the organisation and course of structure of French universities.

37. Raw figures from *The World of Learning 1969–70*, which lists all accredited higher institutions, with enrolment figures.

38. US Office of Education figures, 1970.

39. Speech to the Northern Universities Dinner of the Federation of Conservative Students, Chase Hotel, York, Saturday, 7 March 1970.

40. See L. R. Perry (Ed.), *Four Progressive Educators* (Collier and Macmillan, 1967).

41. See, for example, William Boyd, *A History of Western Education* (Black, London, 1964).

42. See, for example, Jonathan Kozol, *Death at an Early Age* (Penguin, 1967).

43. Mr David Holbrook in particular and the members of Lord Longford's commission on pornography in general.

44. One thing that strikes the visitor to Copenhagen is that the advertising and publicity material outside the sex-shows and in the windows of the sex-shops is in English or German, not Danish. (N.G., personal observations, Copenhagen, September 1971.)

45. Breaking away from authoritarian patterns of classroom teaching is now quite marked, though recent. (Personal observations, R.E.B., Cologne, 1971; N.G., Berlin, 1965 and 1972.) For a pre-war view, see T. Huebener, *The Schools of West Germany* (New York U.P., 1962).

46. The literature on this topic is voluminous, but see Kozol, *op. cit.*, and J. B. Conant, *Slums and Suburbs* (McGraw-Hill, New York, 1961).

47. W. K. Richmond, *Education in the U.S.A* (Alvin Redman, 1956).

48. Calculated from the official curriculum (*uchebnyi plan*) issued by the Ministry of Education.

49. Personal discussions with boarding school staff, Moscow, 1962 (N.G.).

50. *E.g.* Ya. Pilipovskii, 'Sel'skii uchitel' – problemy, suzhdeniya.' *Uchitel'skaya gazeta*, 25 May 1967.

51. Robinsohn and Kuhlmann, *op. cit.*

CHAPTER FIVE

THE ISLANDS OF SAINTED SCHOLARS

There is a great deal to be said for the notion that much of our present difficulty in integrating the various sectors of British tertiary (to say nothing of secondary) education springs from our imprisonment in unexamined myths. As the nineteenth century academics began to put their house in order they depended greatly on appeals to often distant history and precedent; gradually, so great a body of myths grew up to give the respectability of lineage to what was essentially a new, exciting, basically nineteenth-century venture that (in the normal manner of such rationalisations) they took on a reality of their own. That many of the myths were of recent origin, and even mutually contradictory, left them as undeterred as those Christian fundamentalists who insist on believing literally the many contradictions of the first chapters of Genesis. Academics are only human; and if the myths tell them they are the heirs of a glorious tradition stretching back to the Renaissance, not to say the romantic world of Abelard or even Plato, who can be surprised that they fall for such a flattering boost to self-esteem? For two centuries the vast majority of Cambridge dons were almost exclusively given over to the search for ecclesiastical preferment, and until 1800 the Oxford examination system restricted itself almost entirely to discovering whether candidates were gentlemen; but reminding them of this disturbs them no more than any mention of the Borgias will shake an ultramontane Catholic's belief in Papal infallibility.

Such myths have been particularly useful in giving emotive sanction to modern financial priorities. Here is an authentic statement of one who clearly accepts the mythology:

Nevertheless it is true and I must emphasise it, scholarship and research come first. It may seem a harsh thing to say, but a University that sets its sights on the highest level *must* value its scholarship and research above all else. No university *has ever been* or ever can be great by virtue of teaching alone.[1]

It is, of course, perfectly legitimate to assert the priority of research; indeed, it may well be that such a priority lies behind any success that the British university has recently had. But the striking thing is that in thus addressing his General Council, Principal Swann of Edinburgh feels the need for an appeal, not to common sense, but to what he takes to be university *history* in order to back up his assertion. The trouble is that such a notion of university history is sufficiently spurious for it to become a deceptive and disturbing element in any rational attempt to plan tertiary education for the immediate future.

The myth implicit in the Swann assertion was given more startling and dramatic form during a conversation recently overheard in a train from Edinburgh to King's Cross. A female academic, with all the confidence of eight centuries behind her, was, with great patience but also with great vehemence, attempting to cow an unfortunate couple from Lambeth. They had ventured to suggest that their son, a student in Edinburgh, had perhaps been unfairly treated by an offhand professor. 'Oh, but you see,' she explained as if to five-year-olds, 'the universities began as groups of dedicated research workers (the professors?) banding together into communities for the love of learning, and later they were public-spirited enough to allow students into their community, to sit at their feet as apprentices. Students must always remember that.' That professors' aims should be so pure and unsullied by economic considerations would certainly have surprised any Edinburgh professor appointed before 1900, when the size of his income depended directly on the number of students he managed to attract.[2] That they should have seen themselves as dedicated research workers first and teachers second would have seemed equally strange even to Newman[3] and almost every English academic before the 1870s.

Along with this belief in the 'traditional' supremacy of research go a further set of doctrines to which the faithful must defer if they themselves are to enjoy not merely the respect of their colleagues but their own respect of themselves. Thus they must believe, for example, in the mystique of the Academic Community; using the Pauline metaphor (and the religiosity is appropriate), academics are members of one another. They must talk of service to that Community. They must adhere to Newman's 'contagion' theory, whereby setting a professor of chemistry in a close social relationship with a professor of Greek will produce an enlargement of both their world views; that a student of History sharing rooms with a student of Geology will talk of more than sex, games and politics; that, indeed, the two cultures will be bridged and a Coleridgean clerisy of mutually comprehensible educated men will emerge. Requiring an even greater act of faith, they must believe that within this academic community there is a common body of knowledge known as 'academic affairs', so that in Senate or Faculty meetings the professor of one discipline assumes that he can, to the profit of both parties, dabble in the organisational and financial affairs of a quite separate discipline, Thus, a professor of chemistry may even feel that he has more right to an opinion on economics than a graduate student or even a member of the teaching staff (of a lower rank than himself) in economics.

A similar act of faith produces a belief in the reality of 'liberal' education or, more especially, the belief that all subject-matter (whatever its content) can be taught in two ways, 'liberally' and 'illiberally'. To teach a subject liberally – or to assert that it is so taught – fits it for inclusion in the academic canon, no matter how mundane or intellectually undemanding its concerns. A satisfactory definition of 'liberal teaching' is rarely demanded; assertion is all. As it happens, the factors determining a subject's inclusion have usually been economic or sociological. Liberalism is easily discerned in a subject that brings in endowments and research grants. Thus Commerce, Sociology, Education (not to mention medicine, architecture, engineering, or even history and modern languages) were all at one time excluded from the university curriculum on the grounds of their essential 'illiberality'.[4] Their 'liberal' qualities have manifested themselves readily enough as student demand or, later, research grants have justified their being granted respectability.

However, the term 'liberal' is but one of many used to distinguish the work of a 'professor' in a 'university' (generally, and erroneously, believed to be strictly patented terms) from that of teachers in the remainder of the tertiary sector or in secondary schools, crammers, correspondence colleges and all the lower forms of educational activity which 'traditionally' have performed different and less exalted roles.

The university is also, of course, by virtue of its innate and

'traditional' superiority not merely independent of and responsible to no other part of the educational system; it is also by
'traditional' right entitled to freedom from state interference
and from any curb whatever on freedom of speech, creed or
opinions. It is entitled, as Principal Swann puts it, to 'freedom
to teach and publish without censorship, and freedom to make
appointments without political or other interference. In Britain,' he points out, 'these basic freedoms have long since been
won.' He does not define 'long since' but, presumably, in our
traditionally free universities, now under what he sees as un-
wonted financial pressure from government (which shocks him
greatly) it must mean a very long time indeed.

These then are what are believed to be the basic tenets (backed
by centuries of tradition) upon which the 'high qualities' of our
universities depend. Indeed, so widely have they been accepted
that even North American radical students often take them as
historically valid descriptions of a long-established tradition
(even if they see it as one ripe for either renewal or destruction).[5] But if such statements are to remain as basic ingredients
in the rhetorical flourishes of policy-making documents, they
are worth far greater and more serious examination than they
have so far received. They deserve it especially from those academics who in the interests of truth often take pleasure in debunking the quaint myths which non-academics use to cover
the inadequate rags of their rationalisation or the nakedness of
their vested interest. What is sauce for the goose is sauce for the
gander; university history has been strangely neglected until recently by historian and sociologist alike. All too often, deceptive
accounts of historical processes have been allowed to harden,
until their acceptance has itself become part of an academic
package deal.

In fact, so far as Britain is concerned, many of these notions –
the supremacy of research, the belief that the university is traditionally free from outside interference, even the belief that university functions have long since been differentiated from those
of other educational institutions – hardly predate the birth of
people still alive. Nor, until recently, did many universities, save
Oxford and Cambridge, attach any great importance to student
residence,[6] feel any parental duty towards their students, or
even feel any need to disguise the fact that their courses (and,

indeed, their research) took place as a direct response not so much to the inner call of truth as to the needs of society and of those parents or patrons who were willing to pay. Moreover, it was the worst and not the best academics in the nineteenth century who feared state interference, for parliament alone was able to rescue those who valued scholarship from their worst enemies, the majority of their university colleagues.

For although the British university of the twentieth century has been generally right to fight any attempts by the state to interfere in strictly academic matters, it is as well to remember that those in the universities of, for example, 1860 who most valued their academic activities as opposed to their financial interests saw state interference not as aggression but as a true and legitimate defence of their position. As for the notion of the university as the 'traditional' defender of freedom of belief, it would have seemed laughable to the non-conformists and the agnostic scientists who had to fight so long and hard to rescue Oxford, Cambridge and even Durham from Anglican domination.

If the development of the modern British university is examined in a more detached way than hitherto, what emerges is not the picture of a staid, traditional torchbearer passing the light of knowledge from the generations that have gone before, but the far more exciting vision of a new and flexible nineteenth-century creation, the result of a conscious mingling of many ideas from many sources (particularly Germany and America). By examining such *real* traditions, traditions of conscious innovation in response to social and intellectual need, we might well be freed from a cautious guarding of false traditions into a world of continuous and exciting experiment, even with institutional forms. It is ironical that the straitjacket of tradition should have become so tight in an age as full of change as ours; one of our misfortunes, as with the grammar schools, has been to confuse a long *history* with a long tradition.

Some of the habits (though remarkably few) of our modern universities do derive from mediaeval and Renaissance institutions, though usually in the form of nineteenth-century Gothic revivals. Mediæval and Tudor trappings in the shape of the Oxford and Cambridge colleges have survived or been extensively copied, but any real university organisation in both those places was all but dead by 1840 (despite the efforts of a reforming minority of dons) and all attempts at revival met with opposition not from outside, but from the colleges, which rightly saw the resurgence of an overseeing university, with a new wider curriculum and a body of teaching professors, as an economic threat to the vested interests in low-level college teaching.[7]

Reforming ideas came first from Scotland, where the largest universities, Edinburgh and Glasgow, had undergone considerable economic revival as a result of their flexible curriculum and effective catering for the new demand for doctors in the eighteenth century, and because of their refusal to impose religious tests on students. They were also cheaper, demanded no residence, and, unlike the English, did not even place great emphasis on any formal degree structure.[8] They provided models not only for many new foundations in America but also for the major early-nineteenth-century English foundations of a university nature, University College[9] and King's College, London and Owen's College, Manchester.[10] Further, the Scottish universities, like their London and Manchester offspring, found it far easier than did Oxford and Cambridge to adapt more quickly to the direct German influences which were eventually to shame the British university into higher standards of teaching and the hitherto comparatively rare activity of scientific research. They were also open to the influence of Americans such as Jefferson, who were among the first English speakers to appreciate the relevance of the German models to industrial society, and to translate the relevant texts. Indeed, American academics and academic habits (so often seen as purely twentieth-century importations) began to influence British academic thinking at least as early as the 1820s with the publication in London of Jefferson's *Rockfish Gap Report*,[11] just as they were ultimately a major factor in persuading reluctant universities to introduce the Ph.D. degree, an important basis for modern research.[12] In London and even Durham (congenitally prone to following some of the worst Oxford and Cambridge models), those overseas influences were felt very quickly, though even in Scotland, as in Oxbridge, legal difficulties and vested interest sometimes meant that only late in the nineteenth century was there any general acceptance of the university's role as a research institute and a trainer of research students.

It is against such a background, therefore, that the stereotypes must be re-examined, so that many of our 'traditions' begin to emerge not as vestiges of a dim past but as significant new myths created as part of the process of building a university mystique during the late nineteenth century. The ritualism of gowns and ceremonies, of patented titles, an emphasis on legal formularies such as Royal Charters (which have never been necessary for the foundations of a British university)[13] became socially *de rigueur*. The Gothic style of Oxford and Cambridge was adopted in the new buildings, even of such universities as Glasgow, and Scottish ideas for a wider curriculum and greater teaching responsibility, now generally accepted in England, were paid for in models of instant traditionalism. Thus, in at least one Scottish university (where, as at other Scottish universities, few students at the beginning of the nineteenth century bothered to graduate at all) a local tailor appears to have held the copyright of the 'traditional' M.A. hood.[14] The terms 'professor', 'college' and even 'university' came more and more, with no legal basis, to have that exclusiveness which in North America they have still not quite acquired.

Even in contemporary Britain some usages have escaped the net. 'Universities' of dancing have disappeared, but 'colleges' of dancing remain; teachers in Catholic secondary schools still cheerfully and quite legally choose to call themselves 'professors' in just as traditional a style as any university. As late as 1877 a perfectly respectable Glasgow technical college could call itself the Andersonian University without royal charter or mystique, while even the famous 'University of London' of 1824 was seen for a time by Brougham, its leading founder, not as a university in the exclusive modern sense but simply as a London equivalent of the Royal High School of Edinburgh.[15] The Royal High, incidentally, was as late as 1882 vying with Edinburgh University to tempt through its doors the same body of pupils, many of whom chose the University because it was cheaper.[16] Even by 1890 the differentiation of secondary and tertiary education was far from complete. During the late nineteenth century King's College, London found itself not merely teaching old public schoolboys *en route* for Oxford and Cambridge,[17] but also losing pupils to its own preparatory school,[18] which proved a more effective instrument in parents' eyes than the

ostensible 'university', itself founded as an Anglican counter-
blast to Brougham's institution.

This nineteenth-century failure to distinguish clearly between
the functions of universities and other institutions is of crucial
significance. It is related to another phenomenon – the common
belief up to 1950 (but now generally forgotten) that the universities have never formed a homogeneous group sharing similar
aims and status and demanding roughly similar standards of
degree work. As recently as 1883, the question whether the
Scottish universities were in fact secondary schools could be
seriously discussed in philosophical journals such as *Mind*,[19] at
a time when those institutions were filling a role more akin to
that of the modern Further Education College. Until well into
this century, both in Scotland and in London, non-graduat-
ing[20] and part-time university classes were regarded as perfectly
normal phenomena, and until 1900 the taking of honours degrees outside Oxford and Cambridge remained virtually unknown, except by a few post-graduate students.[21] When such
honours graduates as there were passed from Scotland and the
Northern universities to Oxford or Cambridge, it was not to do
post-graduate but undergraduate work, alongside those fresh
from the élitist secondary schools; this division of universities
into leagues was quite acceptable to the Victorians. Thomas
Arnold, in his evidence to the first senate of London University
(the degree-granting, non-teaching state board of 1836, not
Brougham's 'university' of ten years earlier), made it clear that
he saw the new body not as the potential peer of Oxford and
Cambridge but as one performing a quite different function at a
lower level[22] – as, until the end of the century, it continued to
do. Indeed, London University teachers until 1900 were not
even trusted with setting and marking their own students' curricula and examinations;[23] they were essentially 'schoolteachers'
in the eyes of the élitists, or at least potential academics who still
had to make the grade.

But at Oxford and Cambridge themselves the teaching of
undergraduates during the nineteenth century was often at a
level which, as the century wore on, increasingly élitist dons
began to see as more suited to the newly reformed secondary
schools; such schools, for reasons of prestige and scholarship (as
well as to make older boys stay longer) became more and more

anxious to take over what had previously been university work.[24] Even the original Cambridge tripos (or honours examination) was until well into the century always taken at post-graduate rather than undergraduate level. As late as 1880 the Federal Victoria University, formed of three North of England colleges, thought it appropriate to equate the taking of honours with the award of its *post-graduate* M.A. degree; those who had managed to do honours work at the undergraduate stage were excused further examination, and could take their M.A. by payment in the style of Oxford and Cambridge.

Thus, the highly specialised study in depth, now assumed to be the 'traditional' undergraduate degree by many English academics (often so shocked by the continued existence of the broadly based 'shallow' Scottish ordinary degree), was essentially the result of a very gradual drawing of post-graduate work into the undergraduate sector during the nineteenth century.

Moreover, we need to be constantly reminded that the raising of university standards and the widening of the curriculum finally achieved in the mid-nineteenth-century universities was brought about only by the intervention of Parliament. This involved the defeat of a powerful body of academic opinion which even closed the doors of the colleges against reforming Royal Commissions, themselves backed by the Prince Consort, one of the first to appreciate the importance for Britain's future of bringing her tertiary education up to German and American standards. In a similar way, it was the intervention of Parliament in the 1950s which produced the lavish supply of student grants which was so to increase the demand for university places that the universities could institute the rigorous selection procedures which have made them *for the first time* places of generally high academic standards.[25]

Surprisingly recent also is the development of that reputed guarantee of high standards, the tutorial system, traditionally linked in most minds with Oxford and Cambridge. Myth relates this, somewhat glibly, to those fruitful relationships which undoubtedly existed between masters and pupils during the Renaissance, and assumes a largely non-existent continuity between their methods and the tutorial system of the 1970s. By the beginning of the nineteenth century, however, such a close relationship between tutor and pupil had become very rare indeed, judging from the description in the early part of *Apologia pro Vita sua* of the efforts of Newman and his Oriel colleagues to revive it. Such college teaching as there was (and it was mostly poor) took place in largish classes, and at the pedagogical level of schoolmaster and pupil. Newman's idealisation of what he and his fellow reformers tried to do has all too often been taken as a description of some traditional norm, rather than as a commendable exception. Newman's ideal tutor, like his picture of inter-student relationships, was an imaginative creation rather than a typical university phenomenon. The tutor of the early nineteenth century was, above all, concerned with student discipline.[26] He was the schoolmaster in the style of Keate (the great flogger among the headmasters of Eton), and he dealt with what were essentially adolescents. The modern figure who most clearly perpetuates his memory is not the moral tutor of Oxford or the intensive teacher of modern Cambridge supervisions (an invention of the 1880s), but the proctor and his bulldogs, intent on spotting misdemeanours rather than promoting intellectual excitements.

College teaching tended to be carried on not only in large classes but by teachers often far from skilled in either scholarship or pedagogy. Before the 1860s, the university's career structure at both Oxford and Cambridge was that of the Church of England rather than the intellectual world, most of which functioned outside the world of the University altogether in a way that seems remarkable to us nowadays. Even when more intensive intellectual effort came to be required of students, as after the founding of the honours courses at Oxford and Cambridge, much of the intensive teaching was done not by dons in the colleges but by 'private' tutors, in what were essentially 'cramming' situations. Indeed, such 'cramming' tutors could sometimes be dons augmenting their fellowships with extra-mural earnings. It was in such activities, or in the research groups of France or Germany, rather than in any living English college tradition that Newman and his fellow reformers could find models of intensive, high-standard teaching. There is even the ironic possibility that one influence behind the eventual emergence of the one teacher to one pupil relationship at Oxford and Cambridge was an attempt by dons to revive the atmosphere of sessions with research students that they had enjoyed in Germany or Manchester before taking up college appointments.[27]

Jowett and Nettleship's expositions of Plato's *Republic*, with its prescriptions for the training of leaders, achieved an immense vogue. They suited exactly the growing élitist mood of a new academic profession which could no longer tolerate college heads with few intellectual interests[28] and a basic preoccupation with ecclesiastical politics. The dialectic of Plato's dialogue and the wise old man/bright young man relationships of the *Symposium*, alongside the developing example of public school housemasterships, clearly encouraged both greater social intercourse and greater intellectual discussion between tutor and students. The real extent of this new relationship has of course been exaggerated. For decades, generations of Oxford and Cambridge students have regretted that the tutorial system is not what it was. As early as Sir Herbert Butterfield's days as an undergraduate (early days indeed in the actual development of the modern tutorial system), it required considerable rationalisation to defend the surface inefficiency of the tutorial encounter.[29]

From 1870 onwards, however, the élitist pattern began to set. The other universities (including the Scottish), as they attempted to climb the social and economic ladder, began more and more to emulate the outward style of Oxford and Cambridge in the full flush of their economic independence following the new demand for their services during the Imperial period. The traumatic but salutary experiences of state interference in the 1850s and 1860s were behind them. The reorganisation of their finances and their popularity with affluent political or influential alumni made Oxford and Cambridge, unlike their Scottish brethren, almost completely independent of domination by the state or the requirements of the mass student market. It was this feeling, coinciding with a high point of scholarly revival, that gave birth, in pre-Raphaelite or even Wagnerian style, to the myth of the professor with his dedicated scholarship and spiritual independence. The German universities had experienced the same hybris during their own earlier periods of total financial independence, the result of lavish state indulgence. But in Germany the myth had turned sour by 1890, and the decline of academic optimism had made her universities realise that they had no divine right to exist, that ultimately they would be tolerated only if they provided either the expertise or the teaching that society required. The universities are in the perennially precarious position of the artist, dependent either on the market or the patron. Excusably, the English university since 1914 has hardly realised this. It has been in a seller's market and has so taken political approval and patronage for granted that it can almost forget their existence.

On the other hand, the new poverty-stricken Irish university colleges created in the nineteenth century, unattractive to a social élite, depended mainly on attracting poor students and saw the situation somewhat differently. They got their large government grants, but they also got under the Act of 1908 that very supervision of their work by the Comptroller and Auditor General which the Vice-Chancellors now see as a new and sinister threat to academic freedom.[30] Scottish academics also, being less well-endowed than their contemporaries in England, were shrewd enough by the end of the nineteenth century to realise that academic prestige and independence could only exist on a firm financial basis, and increasingly they found that this could most effectively be ensured by providing a veneer for their life as close as possible to that of Oxford and Cambridge. Professors' salaries had been directly dependent on the number of students they could attract, and students were being increasingly attracted by an 'English' (i.e. Oxford and Cambridge) atmosphere. Thus there was a continuous attempt throughout the period from 1850 to 1950 to play up first the superficially mediaeval charm of Edinburgh and St Andrews as suitable homes for 'traditional' universities (though Edinburgh University had not existed in mediaeval times), and, later, the delights of halls of residence.[31] Scottish academics had deliberately rejected these at an earlier period on the specific grounds that such residence was opposed to Scottish academic tradition, divorced students from normal society, and introduced an intolerable element of intrusion into their private lives.

An even greater change in Scotland was the development of the view that students should pursue a coherent specialised course of higher education in one single institution, that they should actually don a gown and graduate, and should, in some sense, owe their institution a more than commercial allegiance. The academic community, with its exclusive rites, strove to replace the more open-doored academic shop. Even so, the force of the Scottish tradition – that the university existed to meet the needs of the surrounding area as well as 'scholarship' – continued as it does today to exert a counter-influence. Even now, the majority of Scottish students (like the majority of London students) live at home, take 'ordinary' rather than honours degrees and see their university training principally as a means of securing adequate employment. What was true of Scotland was also largely true of English universities and university colleges outside Oxford and Cambridge, all of which strove to acquire as much of an Oxbridge 'traditional' veneer as possible, while attracting enough students to keep financially viable. Only with the financial confidence springing from the more generous student grants system in the 1950s did they begin to feel fully the equals of their older rivals, and develop a belief in the 'necessity' of residence as an element of true university experience.

Against this background, it is clearly impossible to see the British universities in their present academically élitist, independent form as anything but the creation of late-nineteenth and early-twentieth-century good fortune – in other words, as a by-product of the hey-day of British industrial and imperial power. That the myths which sustained and stimulated them during such an affluent period should remain unchallenged in present-day circumstances, with the need for less exclusiveness and better teaching as well as more scholarship, seems insupportable. It is a Newmanian myth that demands halls of residence and the isolation of potential graduates from the general community; it is an anti-Newmanian myth which demands the sacrifice of teaching time and resources, where necessary, to the priority requirements of research. It is surely time to examine such 'traditions' to see whether 'the experience of centuries' *has* really justified such practices, or whether they were simply convenient arrangements at a certain stage in our history. Myths usually hark back to golden or heroic ages, but such ages rarely reveal themselves to the historian. At a time when students are increasingly questioning élitist traditions, it is amusing to note that it was one of the true traditions and genuine mediaevalisms, the election of the Rector in a Scottish university by the students themselves, that in 1968 brought Daniel Cohn-Bendit well within striking distance of the Rectorship of Glasgow University and the chairmanship of its main financial committee. Had he succeeded, the irony for the academic traditionalists would, perhaps, have been complete, if somewhat painful.[32]

REFERENCES

1. Address to the General Council of Edinburgh University, 30 January 1969.

2. See, for example, Sir James Barrie's 'An Edinburgh Eleven' (British Weekly, London, 1889), p. 18, where he describes how he chose to attend one professor's classes on the basis of the number of pound notes sticking out of his pocket on the day the fees were paid.

3. The notion that a university is the most appropriate place for the carrying out of high-level research is specifically discounted by Newman in his Idea of a University – a key word for those defending the 'traditional' value system of the university.

4. See, for example, Sir Herbert Butterfield's The Universities and Education Today (Routledge and Kegan Paul, London, 1962), p. 5 passim.

5. In, for example, the writings of Paul Goodman, or in article 'The Humanities and Inhumanities' by Louis Kamps in the Toronto radical journal This Magazine is about Schools, for Winter 1969.

6. Compulsory residence had never been part of the Scottish student tradition. See Marjorie Cruickshank A History of the Training of Teachers in Scotland (University of London Press, London, 1971), p. 102.

7. See D. A. Winstanley, Early Victorian Cambridge (Cambridge University Press, Cambridge, 1940).

8. See A. Morgan, Scottish University Studies (Oxford University Press, London, 1933), which gives evidence of the low incidence of graduation (even by good students) in what were thriving nineteenth-century universities. As late as 1912, a report of the business committee of Glasgow University General Council could begin with the statement, 'In the Faculty of Law it is the exception for students to take any degrees.'

9. H. M. Bellot, University College, London 1826–1926 (University of London Press, London, 1929), pp. 9–11.

10. H. B. Charlton, Portrait of a University 1851–1951 (Manchester University Press, Manchester, 1952), p. 27.

11. H. M. Bellot, op. cit., p. 11.

12. In many cases these were introduced, under some government pressure, at the end of the First World War, not so much for their

own sake as to offer visiting American students the type of research degree they were used to.

13. As the group wishing to found an 'Independent' University discovered recently to their advantage – though, no doubt, also to their astonishment (*The Times*, 22 July 1971).

14. This was only rediscovered when irate graduates later attempted unsuccessfully to prevent its use by the local Art College. He had, of course, responded (in typical tailor fashion) to the developing 'English' taste of Scottish academics as the nineteenth century wore on.

15. H. M. Bellot, *op. cit.*, p. 48.

16. Letter from the Rector of the Royal High School, Edinburgh cited in *Educational News* (Edinburgh, 24 September 1881).

17. F. J. C. Hearnshaw, *The Centenary History of King's College, London* (Harrap, London, 1929), pp. 272–5, 336–9.

18. *Ibid.*, pp. 265 and 325.

19. *Mind*, Vol. III (London, 1877). Article by John Veitch 'Philosophy in the Scottish Universities' pp. 74ff.

'Some people, both south and north of the Tweed, are found in these days not unfrequently to talk and write as if the universities of Scotland were simply large Public Schools of the English type and of a rather inferior sort.'

20. See 8 above.

21. In Glasgow, again, (at that time one of the largest universities in Britain) only four students took Honours degrees in the years 1892–93.

22. See, for example, the views of Thomas Arnold of Rugby in his evidence to the first senate of the University of London.

23. H. M. Bellot, *op. cit.*, p. 380.

24. D. A. Winstanley, *Later Victorian Cambridge* (Cambridge University Press, Cambridge, 1947), Chapter V.

25. It is worth recalling just how low basic entrance requirements, even to Oxford and Cambridge, were before this time and how competition for places was the major impulse for the raising of demands beyond the old School Certificate (the present 'O' level) to that of a set of high 'A' level marks.

26. Even the great Cambridge reformer Whewell was not above indulging in fisticuffs with students in order to restore order in a Cambridge street. See S. Rothblatt, *Revolution of the Dons* (Faber and Faber, London, 1968), Ch. VI, which gives a graphic account of don types and life before and during the reform period. He emphasises how the qualities of amiability or authoritarianism were more likely to characterise early-nineteenth-century dons than was dedicated scholarship of the modern type.

27. See Charlton, *op. cit.* for an interesting general account of the spread of German and American scholarly standards to northern England during the late nineteenth and early twentieth centuries.

28. J. Sparrow in his *Mark Pattison and the Idea of a University* (Cambridge University Press, Cambridge, 1967), pp. 100–101, reminds us that the head of one Oxford college in the 1850s was even reputed to be illiterate until he placed a manuscript notice on the college boards. This, says Sparrow, at least proved he could write!

29. Butterfield, *op. cit.*, p. 5 *passim*.

30. Irish Universities Act 1908 reproduced in T. W. Moody and J. C. Beckett *Queen's Belfast* (Faber and Faber, 1959), p. 789.

31. Plus, at St Andrews, the charms of élitist golf! At the beginning of the 1920s St Andrews catered mainly for local students but thanks to publicity campaigns instituted by Principal Irvine, it had, by 1939, acquired (or re-acquired) a reputation for non-localism and social exclusiveness which is now regarded in Scotland as 'traditional' there.

32. The myth of the student's 'traditional' earnestness of purpose in contrast with the rebelliousness, carelessness and violence of recent years has not been touched on in this chapter but it is, of course, given the lie by a whole range of literature from the novels of the eighteenth century through *The House with Green Shutters*, and *Charley's Aunt*, to Evelyn Waugh's *Decline and Fall* as well as in numerous autobiographies; but one of the more charming testimonies to its inherent contradictions is contained in this extract from a diary item in the *Sunday Times* of 22 March 1970:

(Mr Duncan Sandys) thinks student disorder is linked to ever increasing permissiveness; university Dons ought to send down students who don't behave, but they're too frightened. At Magdalen College, Oxford, when he was a student, he organized a full-scale hoax, sending out 1,000 proctors' summonses to undergraduates. They smashed bottles of whitewash on buildings and called in the Fire Brigade. 'But unlike the students of today,' he says, 'we never claimed the right to run the University, organize the curricula or decide what the exams should be.'

CHAPTER SIX

THE REMARKABLE CASE OF MR TOM BROWN

In recent discussions of the future of secondary education in Britain, all kinds of assumptions have been put about concerning its 'usual' or 'desirable' form, totally obscuring the fact that secondary education, in the form that we know it, has been a relatively recent creation in this country. A typical official curriculum in the secondary school of today, with its wide spread of academic subjects and its emphasis on art, music and, above all, games would have seemed a strange amalgam to the English public or grammar school headmaster of, say, 1820, when classics alone could obtain a place in the *official* curriculum, and where such staple subjects as mathematics (albeit the main subject at Cambridge) and modern languages were relegated to the inferior status of 'extras'. At Shrewsbury School, for example, even mathematics teachers with degrees were not allowed to wear academic dress like their classical colleagues even as late as 1860, and in many grammar schools French was taught not by regular members of staff but by the headmaster's wife or daughter as a means of supplementing their often meagre resources. Games (like life in the dormitories) were seen as belonging to the domain of the boys themselves. Any interference by staff would have been regarded as an unwarrantable intrusion on their personal liberty, and no general attempt was made until the second half of the nineteenth century to incorporate football and cricket (as opposed to gymnastics) into even the 'extra' curriculum, let alone the 'official' one.

However, it is not merely the secondary *curriculum* in England that is of recent origin. Most of the secondary schools themselves are of very recent creation; most of them are, indeed, the secondary modern and comprehensive schools founded since the 1940s to give greater status and scope to the terminal formal education of the majority of the population, hitherto carried on in 'elementary' (*i.e.* extended primary) schools. But what we more easily forget is that even many of the grammar schools that existed in 1960 had no older origins, founded as many of them were from scratch in the late 1940s in order to provide places for the inflated numbers of eleven-year-olds then first given access to them. Even among the longer-established grammar schools, another large group date only from the beginning of this century, artificially created after the 1902 Education Act, when a wide-ranging scholarship system was introduced into England for the first time. And even those grammar schools which date from a much earlier period, the foundations of Tudor times or earlier, had become so educationally moribund by the middle of the nineteenth century that they had to be to all intents and purposes refounded when, after the report of the Taunton Commission in the 1860s, they were put on a sound administrative and educational footing, and their curricula and standards began for the first time to resemble those we know today.

In other words, the typical grammar school of the present is the product not of centuries, but of the past hundred years. Indeed, the foundation or conversion to present educational functions of most grammar schools took place within the memories of people still alive. It is therefore surprising to find the educational correspondent of *The Times*, when the Donnison Commission published its report in 1970, foreseeing great difficulties in changing the grammar schools over to the new routine of the comprehensive school *after centuries* of usage;[1] most of them had already experienced many changes, particularly during the nineteenth century, when the economic pressures of the Imperial period caused secondary schools, like universities, to reorganise themselves radically according to models provided by the American, Scottish and Continental systems.

Even so, many people still see the coming of comprehensive schooling as involving the destruction of the grammar schools' centuries-old 'tradition', and it must be admitted that few of us who attended those grammar schools with centuries of *history* (not quite the same thing as *tradition*) behind them could avoid some emotional pangs at their disappearance. Nevertheless, we must make this essential distinction between *history* and *tradition*, because all too often (as has already been noted in the case of the universities) many fail to see that just because an institution has existed for hundreds of years, this does not necessarily mean that it has been performing the same function or doing the same things during all that period – any more than an eighty-year-old night watchman need be assumed to have been a night watchman all his working life.

Even the continued presence of elements in the curriculum can disguise an essential discontinuity. For example, virtually all ancient grammar schools, throughout the centuries of their existence, have taught Latin; indeed, during some centuries they taught little else. The very name 'grammar school' originally implied this; such a school was meant to provide a grounding in Latin grammar in preparation for those activities to which scholars usually proceeded. Yet the *purpose* of teaching Latin has so altered over the centuries that it is difficult to claim that its continued presence in the curriculum implies any pedagogical tradition at all. Initially, it was a utilitarian subject, as useful in the life of mediaeval Britain (whether ecclesiastical, legal or commercial) as the subjects taught in a technical college are for the everyday life of Britain today.

Only at the time of the coming of Renaissance ideas to Britain in the fifteenth and, even more, the sixteenth century, did Latin and Greek come to be seen as having a primarily cultural significance, guaranteed to widen the mental horizons of the child who studied them. Thus, as those who have seen Robert Bolt's play *A Man for All Seasons* will recognise, a typical Renaissance figure like Sir Thomas More ensured that even his daughter was taught Latin, at a time when the academic education of girls was largely neglected. The role of the classics was to open the minds of the young to the glories of Greece and Rome, and to prepare them for the newly liberated study of philosophy in the universities and rich men's houses of the period.

However, in both grammar schools and universities the realities of teaching unselected and unmotivated pupils (rarely, in either group of institutions, much beyond their mid-teens) forced teachers to fall back on a less spiritually rewarding and more grinding approach to Latin teaching. Despite the lip-service that continued to be paid to the cultural liberation expected from exposure to the classics, they began to realise that only a tiny minority ever got beyond the elementary stages of declension and conjugation; and, given the inordinate time they had to spend on these, the usefulness of such an apparently arid process had to be rationalised in some other way. As a result, learning Latin painfully came to be regarded as a morally worthwhile activity, or a means of 'training the mind' to think clearly. All kinds of inefficient teaching which failed to induce children to learn Latin willingly came to be justified by turning their major defect into a virtue. The painful path of learning Latin became the painful path to mental and moral health, the scholarly counterpart of a painful, exhausting, healthy cross-country run.

The nineteenth century, however, saw a revival of the hopes and cultural justifications of the Renaissance, accompanied by a desire to make the task of learning Latin more congenial and therefore more speedy. Exercises based on the child's own experience were devised, and its relevance was demonstrated. Even so, few pupils encountered much more Latin literature than the easier and more arid passages of Caesar, Livy and Vergil, relying heavily on cheap pre-examination cribs; most teachers have now long since fallen back on justifying the subject's place in the curriculum in terms of its 'mind-training' disciplinary qualities or, less convincingly, of its usefulness in laying a basis for other studies such as modern languages or even spelling. Alternatively, they could until recently shelve the need to justify its place, simply by explaining that it was still required as an entrance qualification by the universities. So the processes of rationalisation and changes of function have gone on, and in these days of 'relevant' curriculum projects some Latin teachers have even begun to justify the study of Caesar on the grounds that he may well be a discussion-starter on such vital interdisciplinary topics as politics and war.

Whatever the legitimate or illegitimate defences may have been for the inclusion of Latin in the grammar school curriculum over the centuries, it hardly constitutes a tradition of challenge, high standards, intellectual activity or even evidence of a traditional routine.

Just as the grammar schools have changed their attitude to Latin as a subject, so as institutions they have been changing their general educational role and status. Like all institutions dependent on attracting custom for their survival, they have naturally had to change their priorities in the search for a satisfactory clientele. In mediaeval times they tended to fill the subservient role of a preparatory institution for those proceeding to universities or to tasks where a knowledge of Latin was essential. During the Renaissance this role was expanded into the more generous one of providing a rounded education for those whose families could afford it, and who preferred schooling to having their children taught at home. A wide curriculum was provided, and high academic standards seem for a time to have been demanded in such new foundations as that of Colet at St Paul's. But over the following centuries, both the curriculum and academic standards generally languished, and there was often a regression to narrower and less worthy aims. The curriculum in particular tended to remain undeveloped, at least officially. This was partly the result of legal impediments in the endowments which prevented the teaching of a wider range of subjects than that envisaged in earlier centuries; but also there were many teachers (as in the universities) who found it convenient to restrict the official curriculum covered by the basic fees (or, in the case of poor boys, by scholarships) so that anything else could be considered 'extra', and charged for accordingly. The result was curricular instability and an uncertain set of curricular values.

Many of the grammar schools, indeed, in the absence of any central government supervision or examinations, declined into mere schools of reading and writing. Others never recovered from the political opprobrium attaching to them at the time of the Civil War, when the grammar schools were often seen as hotbeds of radical thinking. In the case of others, the moral opprobrium attaching to their failure to control the boys' behaviour or their own finances earned many of them a poor, reputation among moralists and among truly educational thinkers. By the end of the eighteenth century, many parents preferred a sheltered education at home or at 'private' institutions to the open life of the public and grammar schools with their uncertain curriculum and standards, their general unruliness (even in 1830 a 'successful' headmaster of Eton could be regularly barracked or even physically attacked during prayers), and their failure to provide a satisfactory general training in a period of commercial, industrial and imperial expansion. Comparisons with America, France, Germany, and perhaps more tellingly, Scotland, convinced the legal and political reformers of the early nineteenth century that the traditional English secondary schools were among the most backward in the European world. The educational initiative temporarily passed to the tutors in the newly founded private schools which gave the parents a curriculum of their choice, or to the pseudo-university institutions such as the Dissenting Academies, the 'University of London', and Owen's College in Manchester (the forerunner of Manchester University), which for many decades provided what was essentially the wide, modern secondary course for older pupils. Indeed, it was not unknown for children to acquire their secondary education in a number of different institutions concurrently (including, possibly, a grammar school and even a university) at a time before educational 'loyalties' or the division between the secondary and tertiary sectors were fully developed.

In the second half of the nineteenth century, even after the work of reorganisation had begun, the curriculum offered in public and grammar schools could still be extremely narrow. The intrusion of such subjects as science, modern languages and geography continued to meet strong resistance, and the Clarendon Commission of 1864 could still remark: 'Natural science ... is practically excluded from the education of the higher classes in England ... This exclusion is, in our view, a plain defect and a great practical evil.'[2] Their view was not shared, however, by those running the schools; as the headmaster of Winchester said in his evidence, 'It is plainly out of the question that we should *teach* chemistry.' The Taunton Commission later in the same decade noted that the great majority of secondary schools in England were just as restricted in their view of what constituted a secondary education as the nine 'great' public schools, and that furthermore they were in most cases teaching it very badly. Clearly, our present notion of public and grammar schools as centres of exciting and wide-ranging scholarship is of a much more recent vintage than many are aware.

So far, we have made little attempt to distinguish the grammar from the public schools – reasonably enough, since any legal boundaries separating them have always been ill-defined. Until the state began to provide financial support for the general mass of grammar schools (and to establish many others) at the beginning of this century, even the social distinctions between them were far from clear. Although Eton and Winchester, because of royal connections, have enjoyed the highest

possible status from their foundation onwards, the status of
others, such as Harrow, Rugby or Shrewsbury, has been much
less clear,[3] for in 1750 (or even in 1800) such schools were
county grammar schools along with all the rest, and their for-
tunes rose or fell with a headmaster's enterprise or failure. Only
with a growing demand for public school places during the
nineteenth century, following the reforms of Temple, Butler,
Arnold and the rest, did the high social status of certain grammar schools become sufficiently established for them to claim to
be the permanent companions of Eton in the ranks of 'public
schools' as the term is now generally understood. By the time
the Clarendon Commission on the Public Schools reported in
1864, only nine (two of them day-schools) were considered to
enjoy such status, and even some of their claims did not go
unchallenged. In the following decades, the closely guarded
membership of such a newly established body as the Headmasters' Conference made it possible for other schools to claim
'public school' status, but the vast majority of the Conference's
members would have had to admit that their claim to such
status was of recent origin. Some, like Oundle, Sedbergh and
Uppingham, had been small-town grammar schools put on the
business map by enterprising headmasters; some, like Clifton or
Marlborough, were nineteenth-century establishments specifically designed to catch the new educational market (Marlborough, apparently, being built near Swindon because it was a
convenient railway junction). Yet others rose to eminence in one
decade and disappeared in the next as their particular market,
or enterprising headmaster, came and went. Most of them were
boarding schools, but some, such as Manchester Grammar or
King Edward's, Birmingham, were primarily not. Social status
could be quickly acquired and then as quickly lost. The schools,
in fact, existed not in two clear groupings – public schools and
the rest – but on a continuum, up and down which all but the
most established moved. The reasons for such movements varied
enormously – the enterprise of a headmaster, a cut in fees, a
court case, a successful cricket team – only on some occasions a
curriculum change or academic success.

It is not surprising, therefore, that by the time the Fleming
Committee met in the 1940s to discuss the future of the 'public
schools', definition of the term still proved difficult – especially

as membership of the Headmasters' Conference (previously a rough and ready guide to current status trends) now embraced a number of local authority day grammar schools (elected on the strength of their 'antiquity' or connections with Oxford and Cambridge) which could not by any stretch of the imagination fit the journalistic category of 'public schools' as it existed in the minds of most Englishmen.

In fact, most Englishmen have a great tendency to divide institutions of secondary education into categories that have little basis in reality but are highly potent in their effect on their educational thinking. Upper-middle-class Englishmen, for example, think for the most part of independent, socially prestigious 'public schools' on the one hand (what most of them think of as 'good' schools) and publicly financed, inferior and often ill-mannered state schools on the other. In fact, of course, there are many well-known schools that fit into neither category – particularly the direct grant schools, independent and socially prestigious but publicly financed and admitting a large proportion of state scholars. There are also many independent schools – experimental ones like Summerhill or Monkton Wylde, or cut-price institutions offering a grammar-school type of education to 'eleven-plus failures' – which would not or could not claim to be prestigious in either a social or academic sense.

Nevertheless, the potency of glib dichotomising has dominated a remarkable amount of English thinking about secondary education since the Second World War. This is not surprising, for the grammar schools since then have seemed to offer aspiring parents a haven where their children could be firmly and cheaply on the state side of the fence and yet not of it, sharing through grammar school 'tradition' in the world of the rich man's public school, with its reputedly high academic standards, its cultural tone, its good manners and its promise of great opportunities ('giving the clever child a chance'). Such was, indeed, the rationale of 'eleven-plus' support in the Labour Party at one time – opening the world of the rich to the deserving poor.[4] Of course, it was erroneous to think of the grammar schools as forming a homogeneous group at all; there has always been just as wide a continuum of standards and prestige among them as among the public schools themselves. But in an educational world more and more given to thinking in terms of journalistic dichotomies of good and bad, high and low, upper class and lower class, it is not surprising that the high status public school and high status grammar school should come together as allies, as both saw their 'high standards', academic and social, threatened by state educational policies which menaced public school independence on the one hand and advocated comprehensivisation on the other.

Both had in any case been conceived with a similar academic purpose, and the modern grammar schools had almost without exception modelled themselves enthusiastically on their public school 'superiors'. Indeed, many of the state-founded grammar schools had been deliberately planned on public school lines by inspectors and headmasters who, as so often happened, were themselves public school products or regretted that they were not. They knew of no other acceptable models of secondary education but the late-nineteenth-century public schools with their immensely high social prestige and 'obvious' qualities as seminaries for 'leaders'.

In such circumstances, it is salutary to remember that in both groups of schools before the Second World War, no universally high standard of entry was ever required. To the public schools were admitted the children of the social élite, on the whole regardless of ability, with the so-called 'common entrance' examination providing a minimum rather than an optimum test of attainment in the basic subjects; its 'pass-mark' was a matter for *ad hoc* decision by a particular school rather than something universally valid. To most of the grammar schools (despite their putative role as providers of education for the penniless but able) fee-paying pupils spanning the full range of ability were freely admitted, regardless of academic promise or, in some cases, their degree of literacy.[5]

Only in the years immediately after the war, with the growth of a new insistence on academic ability as the key to success in an increasingly meritocratic society, did the demand for places at 'good' schools so increase that public schools were compelled to raise their entrance requirements, while the grammar schools were for the first time compelled to restrict their entry to those 'passing' the eleven-plus.[6] Yet this was hardly seen as a return to true grammar school 'tradition' by the grammar school teachers themselves. One grammar school headmaster at the time, Alec Peterson (now head of the Oxford Department of Educational Studies) has noted how so many of his colleagues continually deplored the attempt to turn their old tolerant schools into mere nurturers of academic ability at the expense of boys of 'character' (*i.e.* the less able fee-payers), while public school old boys complained bitterly as each school in its turn began to turn its back on their children because of failure in some silly examination or psychological test.

In other words, the traditional appeal of the public and grammar schools seems to lie not in academic qualities but in some kind of 'social tone' which they are supposed to have acquired over the ages. What in the middle of the nineteenth century was a heterogeneous collection of sometimes philistine and often riotous establishments has now come to be seen as sharing some common 'traditional' qualities of 'order' and 'standards'. How did such a belief gain such wide currency so quickly?

It was partly a deliberate artifice; it was what schools with an eye to the main chance wished people to believe. Governing bodies and public school headmasters were on occasion quite capable of consciously creating traditions overnight.[7] Thus, the reformers of moribund Rugby at the beginning of the nineteenth century chose to house it in artificially ancient-looking buildings (possibly modelled on Eton) because these were considered more appropriate for school activities, just as even the Board Schools founded after 1870 for the children of the poorest members of society were very often built to a few standard designs sent out from Whitehall – all of them 'Gothic' or 'Tudor', since these were considered to provide a suitably academic atmosphere. Similarly, as in the universities, a new emphasis came to be placed on the wearing of academic dress and on the minutiae of 'ancient' rituals, many of them (like the National Eisteddfod of Wales) romantic revivals unknown in the easy-going days of the eighteenth century.

The creation of a ritual and mythology to which the status-seeking newly reorganised (or newly founded) schools could refer for the derivation of their 'traditions' became as profound and far-reaching as the cult of the American West. Just as the characters and manners of the West's early days underwent considerable idealisation (with such figures as Jesse James and

Wyatt Earp taking on a persona and significance far removed from reality), so the great heroes of school reform – Arnold in particular – underwent apotheosis at the hands of their followers. Just as certain modes of life in the West which lasted a few years at most became preserved in the art forms of a popular world culture, so the procedures of certain leading public schools in the last decades of the nineteenth century established themselves as a norm of 'good' school behaviour and values through the school stories read by hosts of British schoolboys for the next fifty years and more – even after many of the procedures had become irrelevant, and the social conditions which produced them had long since passed away.

Scholars are some way from fully understanding such an interrelationship between popular literature and great social movements. Rather than simply mirroring such movements, some myths (however obviously literary) seem on occasion to accelerate or even to change the shape of the movements they ostensibly reflect. Did the American drive to the West give rise to the cult of the Western novel, or was the cult of the Western novel one factor in reinforcing the underlying enthusiasm for the drive? Certainly, the school stories of P. G. Wodehouse and of best-selling weeklies such as the *Magnet*, the *Gem* and, later, the *Rover*, *Hotspur* and *Wizard* must (on the evidence of numbers) have been read by millions (outside the ranks of the public schoolboys) who could not readily identify with their heroes, just as 'society' romances were read largely by working or lower-middle-class girls. Yet who knows what conditioning effect such a diet of exciting and highly ritualised apologiae for élitist forms of schooling must have had, not only on English educational thinking in general but even on the élitist school themselves? Certainly, aspiring state grammar school headmasters at the turn of the century soon began to refer to their school certificate failures as the 'Remove', and words like 'Shell' and 'Prefects' began to appear in old-established but low-status schools where they had been unknown before.

In his essay on 'Boys' Weeklies',[8] George Orwell has examined closely this peculiarly English phenomenon of the cult of the school story. In suggesting that it may have saved English industrial society from bloody revolution through making the ruling class seem so delightful to the working-class boy during his formative years, he also hints at a more conscious use of school fiction as a direct means of social control by establishment figures. He sees it both as legitimising upper-class norms and prestige in working-class eyes and as a purveyor of upper-class values and forms of self-discipline to the population as a whole; and, of course, for such evangelical tasks, the degree to which there was any relationship between such fiction and reality was of only secondary importance. Indeed, too much reality might well be a hindrance to its efficacy.

Nowhere, however, does this gulf between fiction and reality become clearer than in the cult of Thomas Arnold as the Greatest of All School Reformers. There is, of course, no doubt that Arnold was a significant figure in the history of the public schools, but the nature of his real role has undergone considerable scrutiny in recent years, particularly at the hands of Bamford, his most recent biographer.[9] For him, Arnold is merely one in a line of Rugby reformers, but one with a special flair for attracting publicity, not all of it favourable, and a special interest in developing the sixth form and sixth formers. Generations of Englishmen, on the other hand, have encountered Arnold largely through the pages of *Tom Brown's Schooldays*,[10] and on the basis of the congenial and wise figure presented there has been erected a myth of a charismatic figure whose views and story are recounted as if they were the views and story of a Christ or Buddha. His devotees have their own Annunciation story, in which Hawkins of Oriel prophesies that if Arnold is appointed to Rugby he will change the face of education throughout English public schools.[11] In one sense, Arnold did this very thing, but Bamford asks us to consider how. He sees him not as a great secondary teacher but as a something less than totally dedicated schoolmaster whose major interests lay outside the school in the fields of political, religious and university reform,[12] who left the school on the afternoon of the last day of term and never returned until the first day of the following one,[13] whose period at Rugby was far from free of public scandal, and who by some criteria may actually have left the school in a worse state than he found it on taking over from an undoubtedly reforming and efficient predecessor. Bamford questions our belief in Arnold as the great prophet of boarding[14] (he seems to have believed that day-schools were superior, based as they were on the family), of games (in which he seems to have had little interest as a means of discipline), of the stiff upper lip (his sermons were highly emotional and encouraged repentant boys to weeping and emotionalism in return) and, above all, of pastoral care (judging from Bamford's account of some of his dealings with boys who were clearly in need of counsel).[15]

Yet, Bamford insists, Arnold had an enormous influence on his fellow headmasters. How then did this happen? Some of them were, of course, his own pupils, though not all of those who became teachers seem to have followed in his steps too closely. Instead, his influence seems to have been mediated not so much through people as through books, two in particular – Dean Stanley's Life[16] and Hughes' Tom Brown's Schooldays. These two, though both written by passionate admirers of Arnold, are remarkably far from complementing each other. Stanley, seriously concerned with disseminating what he saw as Arnold's best moral, political and educational ideas, is said to have been astonished, even appalled, by Hughes' portrait.[17] Hughes seemed, he said, to have been writing of a totally different Rugby from that which he had known as Hughes' contemporary, just as Stanley himself is in Bamford's view writing of an Arnold impossibly idealised and remote from reality. Yet these two varied pieces of wishful thinking underlay much of the ritual formation and mythology of English élitist education in both public and grammar school until probably half-way through this century. The values of Tom Brown and of the hundreds of genre novels and weeklies which sprang from it still, perhaps incredibly, tend to provide norms of educational 'goodness' even for those generations of Englishmen who are still alive and still engaged in current controversy.[18]

Such norms were, of course, originally acceptable because they answered exactly the upper- and middle-class needs both of a world-wide empire and English industrial society at a particular stage of its development. In particular, they provided colourful procedures for differentiating élitist education from that of the lower orders. The myths created were exceptionally deep and powerful ones, as the continuing cult of the school story demonstrates; and while such myths may now only appear (as the Western myth now tends to appear) in a debased form –

for example, in the psychological probing of William Trevor's *The Old Boys*,[19] or in the straight debunking of *St Trinian's* or *Whacko* – outright rejection is slow in coming. Moreover, the institutions which embody such popular myths, and their accompanying value systems, cannot be destroyed lightly, any more than the American gun laws which arose from and buttressed the Western myth can be set aside lightly. Indeed, one central myth – that of the centuries-old search for the Grail of 'high standards' – has achieved a new and potent significance during the past two decades, during which the public and grammar schools have adopted their new and more 'relevant' role as nurturers of the academically excellent in a complex technological society.

The irony is that such an academically sophisticated role lay far outside the dreams of those who led the reform movement of the nineteenth century. Their Grail was far more often that of high moral tone and self-discipline of 'service' than that of striving for high academic standards. It was certainly far from the dreams of the flogging headmasters found so often in the Chronicles of Eton or in the pages of Lamb's essays, few of whom had any illusions about their boys' academic potential, and who saw their task as a grim and literally bloody one. The quest for excellence might even have offended the truly major reformer of English pedagogy in the nineteenth century, Thring, the founder of the Headmasters' Conference; he saw his task at Uppington as the deliberate avoidance of the cult of the able at the expense of the less able, and emphasised that the school had a prime duty towards its more backward pupils[20] – hardly a characteristic concern of the grammar schools known to most of us, where all but the top stream (even of such a highly selected entry) are treated as actual or potential 'failures'.

A Personal Note[21]

To end this chapter, it might be useful to examine in rather more detail how one English grammar school with a long *history* stretching over many centuries won and lost a whole set of élitist *traditions* during a mere hundred years or so before sinking to a peaceful non-élitist end as part of a comprehensive school during the 1960s. The school in question is, in fact, the

one which the author of this chapter himself attended and he
freely admits that such were the great myths' hold upon him
that, despite the fact that he already had access to much of the
information and held many of the views elaborated in this chapter, he could still feel pangs at the 'destruction' which comprehensivisation threatened to bring to his old school. His early
conditioning to 'traditional' views was still strong enough to
hold him emotionally, even after he had long abandoned any
belief in their historical basis. What were these powerful traditions and what was the truth behind them?

In fact, the historical claims made for this particular school
were quite considerable ones. The documentary evidence of its
existence was uncontestable for the period since Henry VIII's
reign. At that time, as happened with so many schools during
the reformation period, it became a 'new foundation', one of the
Cathedral grammar schools put on a sounder footing in order
that there would be at least one satisfactory Latin school in each
diocese and in order that there would be at least one centre for
training aspirants to the new, reformed priesthood. However,
there is little doubt that a grammar school of sorts had already
existed for a considerable period and no reason to doubt that it
dated back at least to the Cathedral's own foundation in the
twelfth century. During that period it must, indeed, have been
the only real *institution* of literate education in the city. Nineteenth-century tradition-mongers, however, pushed its origins
even further back. On the basis of a slight reference in Bede's
History of the English People to the establishment of 'a school'
in the city during the visits of St Cuthbert, they saw the very
same school already rearing its head through the somewhat extensive mists of the seventh century. Hey presto! The Grammar
School of 1890 knocked even Eton into a cocked hat so far as
'tradition' was concerned – it had existed for thirteen centuries
in comparison with Eton's puny five or less. That no one could
describe the content of that tradition for more than half of
those centuries mattered not at all.

Yet even during the period since Henry's refoundation, the
school had undergone considerable vicissitudes – sufficient to
cast doubt on the notion of its having a continuous, academic
'tradition' of high standards. Indeed, in the eighteenth and early
nineteenth centuries, it had shrunk to almost nothing – existing

in a small upper room in the Abbey gateway, with a master and a mere handful of scholars of, to say the least, varying abilities and heterogeneous social origins. Clearly it took every pupil it could get.

The revival of the public schools in the mid-nineteenth century gave it new vitality – not only in its own right but as a place where the sons of local gentry and tradesmen could prepare themselves for entry to the reformed public schools proper, while the bulk of its pupils filled lowly posts elsewhere (many of which would hardly demand a grammar school training) or, if they were intending to be clergy, sat at the master's feet in the grinds provided after school and scrambled for the few Oxford scholarships that were available.

Only after the Taunton Commission in the 1860s cleared the way for the establishment of a proper secondary system by devising machinery for the reorganisation of endowed schools' tasks did the school begin to build up an academic, and social, reputation of its own. The establishment of scholarships for student teachers gave it a further (though socially dubious) intake. In a period of *instant 'tradition'* its historical background and Cathedral connections helped considerably in its search for commercial viability, but at no point did it become either socially or intellectually exclusive. Ironically, social exclusiveness seems to have only been assured in this century, after the establishment of more widespread county scholarships, for (as is well known) a remarkable number of scholarships tended to go to the children of middle-class parents who, seeing a new and healthy intellectual competition in the school, were more inclined to patronise it than might have been the case before. By 1930 a particularly enterprising, tradition-laden headmaster had at last made the school commercially and intellectually viable partly and ironically (as was the case with so many successful headmasters) by adding what was almost itself a traditional if paradoxical element in the public school, the extra spice of original 'untraditional' eccentricities of his own. For example, his pacifist views compelled him to abolish the prestigious Officer Training Corps in favour of Boy Scouts, while, for a time, he suspended the holding of formal classes in favour of the American Dalton plan, which granted boys considerable autonomy in the planning of their personal time-tables. He was, in fact, educationally more successful when, like Thring, he combined the search for synthetic historical tradition (typically, he commissioned a Memorial Register – the ritual display of tradition – compiled by the historian of Marlborough and he approved a highly racialist school song) with a genuine originality and educational enterprise involving a rejection of *pedagogical* tradition. Suffice it to say that, in the end, the school was admitted to the Headmasters' Conference – presumably on the basis of examination success and – even more – of its 'ancientness'. At all events, the new-found high prestige was sufficiently buoyant for these to be the cause of tension in the 1940s over whether the school should move wholeheartedly into the newly reorganised state system (thus shedding all feepayers and their accompanying social prestige) or opt for semi-independence as a direct grant school. 'Tradition' (all thirty years of it!) was seen as threatened if the school were merged into what was generally assumed to be the drab, bureaucratic greyness and low standards of the local authority system. In school magazine editorials of the time the author of this chapter personally said so. But, alas, 'tradition' fell, and fee-payers (though through a quirk of meritocracy, not the school's social status!) melted away. The path to comprehensivisation was made certain, though, ironically, the 'tradition' apparently destroyed in 1944 was mysteriously resurrected before being used in the final fight to the death.

Yet who could deny now that the Comprehensive which emerged is just as entitled to be counted the descendant of St Cuthbert's original town school, the repository of the city's educational tradition, as the grammar school ever was?

REFERENCES

1. Brian McArthur wrote: 'Among the arguments constantly reiterated (before maintaining the present direct grant system) were the need to preserve variety within the National Education System; the aims of the schools' founders were usually to provide an academic education; the big catchment areas served by the school, often covering more than ten education authorities; and the difficulty of adapting to comprehensive education after a centuries-old tradition of academic education; and the smallness of the schools.' *The Times,* 26 March 1970.

2. The Clarendon Report, 1864, quoted in J. Stuart Maclure, *Educational Documents, England and Wales 1816–1969* (London, Methuen, 1969), pp. 85–6.

3. See for example the amusing exchange of letters between the cricket captains of Shrewsbury and Westminster in the Fleming Report of 1944 (Appendix A).

4. For an interesting and detailed discussion of the party's changing attitudes see R. Barker, *Education and Politics 1900–1951: A Study of the Labour Party* (Oxford University Press, 1972).

5. See the account of the hero's schooldays in George Orwell, *Coming up for Air* (Penguin, 1962).

6. It is worth remembering that the number deemed worthy of passing varied enormously – from some 10 per cent in Gateshead to more than 40 per cent in nearby Westmorland. The process clearly depends more on the number of places readily available than on any 'grammar school level of ability'.

7. In a BBC Further Education broadcast.

8. George Orwell, 'Boys' Weeklies', *Horizon 3*, March 1940; this is available in paperback in *Inside the Whale and Other Essays* (Penguin, 1962).

9. T. W. Bamford, *Thomas Arnold* (London, Cresset Press, 1960).

10. Thomas Hughes, *Tom Brown's Schooldays* (1857).

11. See Bamford, *op. cit.*, pp. 19–20.

12. *Ibid.*, p. 148.

13. *Ibid.*, p. 117.

14. *Ibid.*, pp. 108 ff.

15. *Ibid.*, p. 188.

16. Dean A. P. Stanley, *Life and Correspondence of Dr. Arnold* (1944).

17. Bamford, *op. cit.*, pp. 78–9.

18. Bamford writes: 'The growth of the legend and the reasons behind it are clear. Arnold himself, Oxford and the Newmanites, Stanley, Tom Brown, Rugby football – all these and more form a sequence of building up Rugby as the key school in the middle years of the nineteenth centry. The public desire to fasten reforms on to individuals found fulfilment in Arnold himself, the one headmaster of the period who happened to be a man of real consequence outside the classroom.

Unfortunately for the legend, the reforms which we now regard as most worthwhile – the reduction of flogging, courtesy instead of brutality among boys, the disappearance of classical rickets in a widening of the curriculum – had nothing to do with Arnold; while his own particular insistence on the clergyman-master as a curator of souls, the power of a flogging sixth and an intense religious attitude among boys, have gone altogether.' (Bamford, *op. cit.*, p. 189.)

19. William Trevor, *The Old Boys* (Penguin, 1966).

20. See T. W. Bamford, *The Rise of the Public Schools* (London, Nelson, 1967), p. 70.

21. This is by R. E. Bell. The evidence is drawn partly from personal reminiscence and interviews, partly from G. B. Routledge, *Carlisle Grammar School Memorial Register, 1264–1926* (Carlisle, Thurnam, 1926), which contains an 'historical sketch' by the headmaster.

CHAPTER SEVEN

THE USES OF MYTHOLOGY

The *Concise Oxford Dictionary* defines myth as 'a purely fictitious narrative, usually involving supernatural persons, etc., and
embodying popular ideas on natural phenomena etc.; fictitious
person or thing'. For our present purposes, this definition is at
once too narrow and too broad. Not all fictitious persons, things
or narratives are myths, and it is probably stretching things
rather far to equate myth with simple error. Contrariwise, myth
need not be *entirely* fictitious: as we have seen, many current
assumptions about education do contain a good deal of fiction,
but there is normally an element of fact as well. They are not
'purely fictitious', nor are they concerned with 'supernatural
persons etc.', though as they are presented some of the principal
personalities come pretty close. But much of the familiar body
of myth of the more recognisable sort – classical and the like – is
now generally agreed to contain some factual material. The Trojan War has already been offered as an example of this, and
many others spring to mind, such as the legend of Theseus and
the Minotaur with its obvious echoes of Minoan Crete, or the
inflation of the defeat of Charlemagne's rearguard by the
Basques into the epic Christian–Muslim confrontation of the
Chanson de Rolland. What makes them mythical is the treat-
ment, the intrusion of the fictitious, the irrational and even the
magical into an ostensibly factual account or explanation; and
in this respect much current thinking on education can be fairly
described as mythical.

Myths, ancient and modern, are of various kinds. There is
heroic epic, like the *Iliad, Beowulf,* or the legend of Thomas
Arnold (now brought to the ultimate in ritual drama in a television serial and a stage musical). There is the evocation of a
Golden Age, whether one looks for it in Hesiod, Ovid or the
numerous accounts of a glorious past of freedom in the universities and grammar schools so nostalgically brought up in practically every generation. There are the tales of cataclysmic doom,
like the Norse *Ragnarökr* (the Twilight of the Gods, to give the

more familiar Wagnerian title), or the grim forebodings of the authors of the Black Papers. And, of course, there are innumerable creation myths, from the Babylonian *Enuma Elish* to the filling of the Yawning Gap by the more recently arrived Norse gods; education equivalents include the widespread belief that the Scottish educational system sprang fully-armed from the head of John Knox,[1] but there are plenty of others.

The trappings of myth have their parallels too. Anyone can with some ease construct pantheons or demonologies according to taste. As we have seen, the accounts of what goes on in other countries (in accuracy and in function) bear a close resemblance to travellers' tales, whether of the Eldorado or monster-populated desert variety. There are the rituals, the invocations of ancestral spirits, the incantations and repetitions of magic formulae, the prophylactic gestures and amulets, the superstitions – using again the *Concise Oxford* definition of superstition as including 'irrational fear of the unknown or mysterious; misdirected reverence'. Indeed, if Graves is right, 'true myth may be defined as the reduction to narrative shorthand of ritual mime performed at public festivals, and in many cases recorded pictorially'[2] – not a bad summary of some university and school history, and the actions based upon their being taken literally.

Apart from supplying some colour (and possibly some comfort), myths have two main functions – to explain, and to justify. As cosmogonies, they offer an account of how things got to be the way they are – the stars are bright because Odin puts sparks from Muspelheim in the sky to light it, 'public' schools have developed as élite institutions from early times, and so forth. Such accounts also glorify the creators – Zeus, Odin, Marduk, Plato, Arnold, Knox or even whole social classes (thus rivalling the gods of Egypt and India in strength of numbers). By extension, they can be used to legitimise things as they are – the High King of Mycenae claimed descent through Perseus from Zeus himself and therefore divine authority for his position; the universities are thought to represent a long-established and continuous concern for disinterested scholarship and academic excellence, and therefore claim intellectual and traditional authority for theirs.

Myth thus serves a purpose much wider, and much more serious, than mere embellishment; it can become an ideological or conceptual shorthand, obscuring the need for argument, analysis or definition, especially (as is so often the case) when it is suffused with a general feeling of awe. In this atmosphere, logical leaps are understandably frequent. One of the striking things about the Fleming Committee's reliance on Shakespearian rhetoric (already quoted; see p. 22) is the use of the word 'therefore' to switch from vague high-flown musings to a concrete assertion concerning the transfer of children from primary to secondary schools. Not only is the logical connection absent, but its absence is not even noticed. Similarly, when the Secretary of State for Education and Science declared[3] that 'good' schools must be preserved in local authority reorganisation schemes, there was no attempt to define 'good', still less to justify the equation of 'good' with 'selective'. Selection is controversial, but we are all in favour of good schools; attempts at definition would, of course, produce some widely differing views of what this meant, with differing criteria and priorities. By keeping the discussion at a vague level, and by using 'good school' as a reverential rather than a descriptive term, the highly dubious assumption that selection is an essential part of this goodness slips into the conclusions. It is not really an argument at all, but rather an exercise in sustaining belief in the rightness of things as they are. In the same way, the antiquity of a school (or a category of schools) may be invoked against attempts to reorganise its relations with the rest of the educational system. We have already seen how much of the 'tradition' is instant rather than real, and that very few of even the old schools have enjoyed their present position or filled their present roles since their foundation. One might even suggest that there is a good case for regarding the entire school system for a given area as the legitimate descendant of the particular grammar or grant-aided school in question. But this is not the essential point; logically, the only reply to pleas about a school's antiquity is 'so what?' If *other* arguments can be adduced for keeping an existing institution in its present form, well and good; but it is hard to see how antiquity alone, even if genuine, can be allowed to over-rule all other considerations (which is what such pleas amount to). Even in an allegedly tradition-loving country as Britain, few voices are raised in favour of reviving trial by combat, witch-burning, bear-baiting or similar picturesque customs on grounds of their lengthy pedigree alone. These examples may seem absurd, but the logic is the same.

If this seems no more than a statement of the obvious – 'good reasons must of need give place to better' – it is worth noting how often the antiquity argument *is* brought out to stand (often rather shakily) without visible means of support from any other kind of argument. And when this argument is resisted, the temperature rises to a heat of language more appropriate to expressions of horror at sacrilege than an attempt to conduct a discussion. Almost any report of a town council or parliamentary debate on the subject, or the correspondence columns of almost any newspaper, will supply examples in plenty. Those in search of real collectors' pieces may care to consider an attempt by Esmond Wright, a former Glasgow M.P., to link the motives of supporters of comprehensive schools with the impulse to vandalism so noticeable in that city,[4] or this gem from Charles Graham in the *Scottish Daily Express* on the moves to stop fee-paying in *local authority* schools and integrate them in a comprehensive system:

Are we seriously asked to take our government, our rulings, from Docherty and Mains, regardless of the statutory deficiency of their plans, of the unguarded disapproval of the Secretary of State for Scotland? The campaign against the (selective fee-paying) schools has always been one of hate, a policy basically doctrinaire and latterly vicious. Now in the face of rejection (by the Secretary of State) it becomes anarchistic and flies in the face of all democratic precepts and principles. The one happy result being the more likely preservation of the schools that are now being lawlessly attacked. The Labour men have shown their true colours. And they are ugly.[5]

One could point out that since the council (including Docherty and Mains) *has* been democratically elected, and that since it is charged by law with organising education in the city (subject to the approval of the Secretary of State, who in this case 'unguardedly' disapproved), words like 'anarchistic' and 'lawless' hardly apply, whether one agrees with the policy or not. The policy is, of course, highly controversial and the legitimate subject for a great deal of argument on ends and means alike. But the notable thing about this piece, and many others like it, is not the argument, for there is none; it is the tone. This particular piece is, perhaps, a little extreme in being rather more violent (and more shaky grammatically) than most; but the alogicality, the use of outrage in place of argument, is typical enough, and a reasonable indication of the power of myth to obscure discussion in present times no less than in the past. In fairness, though, it must be pointed out that this kind of thinking is not entirely a monopoly of the educational Right; a considerable number of reformers seem prepared to accept as educationally and socially virtuous any school to which the label 'comprehensive' may be attached, even if local circumstances (especially in cities with many socially homogeneous areas and/or a substantial independent sector creaming off the state schools) ensure that they are nothing of the kind.

If ancestor-worship (or, at the other end of the political scale, 'whoring after strange gods') is common, so is the ritualistic use of language. We have already seen a few examples of this; but it is not confined to occasional outbursts of wrath at the defiling of sacred objects. Much of the language of educational pronouncement (one hesitates to say 'discussion') has other affinities with ritual and myth. Favourites are the assertion of alleged truths backed up with repetition, a technique favoured by Mr Enoch Powell among others. ('There is no, repeat no justification' for the participation of students in the government of universities[6] – no argument, just reiteration.) At this level, the sermon – judgements delivered by the priest to the people – is the appropriate parallel, not the exchange of argument among equals. Again, there is the ritual incantation, the solemn utterance of approved phrases in a manner intended to evoke favourable responses rather than in any semantically analysable way. This is not to say that the much-used hooray-words are in themselves devoid of semantic content, but that their use is. This is true of ritual of the more familiar kind as well; practically any utterance in the ritual of any creed uses words which in other contexts do have examinable meanings, except that this does not greatly illuminate their ritual use, and may even be hostile to it. Defenders of ritual who are aware of this may make the point that the words have symbolic rather than literal meaning, which is fair enough within the context of the general structure of the faith in question. The trouble with ritual language in education is that this necessary distinction is not recognised. Words like 'freedom', 'good', 'high-level', 'progressive' and so forth are thrown around in such a way as to claim rational force for what is essentially an incantatory usage; or, to put it another way, language used in ritual for the faithful masquerades as rational argument addressed to the world at large.

One of the favourites in current controversies over selective versus comprehensive schooling is 'freedom of choice'. In a society which makes much of individual freedom this phrase has an obvious appeal; and, of course, it is also open to semantic examination. The trouble is that its meaning is far more complex – and debatable – than its casual use might suggest, and that it is extremely doubtful that it will bear the construction placed upon it by those most given to its use. For as it happens, 'freedom of choice' is the principal watchword of the defenders of selective and in particular fee-paying selective schools, but its applicability is by no means clear. If 'freedom of choice' means the right to send one's children to schools outside the national system, then it could be claimed to have some force, though clearly it is a freedom reserved to a small and relatively wealthy minority. But when it is applied to semi-independent or publicly maintained schools it becomes altogether more dubious. It is perhaps possible to argue that the public (and the taxpayer) should directly or indirectly maintain an élite sector limited to those who can get by the academic and/or financial hurdles; it might be possible to argue that even if this does convey special benefits and privileges on a minority, society at large benefits from the spin-off. What is rather harder to see is how 'freedom of choice' can be used to justify a type of school which is distinctive in keeping large numbers out – that is, by denying a similar 'freedom of choice' to others. To make any kind of logical sense, the definition of freedom would have to be redrawn, making it clear *whose* freedom is involved, and finding another set of arguments to justify the exercise of this freedom by one group of people at the expense of that of another group. Short of putting it bluntly as 'freedom of choice for *me*' it is hard to see what form such a definition could take. This, of course, sounds uncomfortably like pleading for special privilege with no special justification, which few are prepared to do (at any rate openly); yet this is what 'freedom', *in this usage*, boils down to. (Historians may care to recall that the various movements to defend 'liberties' by barons against kings, city corporations against central governments, parliament against king, and the like, were emphatically not concerned with liberty in the abstract, but with protecting certain group privileges from encroachment from higher up – and lower down.) The notion that 'freedom is indivisible' has been allowed to confuse the issue, but logically there is no reason why it should. Now, a case can be made for privilege; to a limited extent, most governments of all complexions already accept it, given that university education is still a privilege limited to a minority, but one which most governments are prepared to underwrite in view of the assumed benefits to society from the skills and expertise of this minority. In the case of the élite schools, however, this is not generally the case that is made. The appeal to 'freedom of choice' in this context is no case at all, and it is doubtful if it is really intended as such. It is a ritual blessing – and, in many quarters at least, quite an effective one.

It might be objected that even if many beliefs about education are myths, even if it is beset by superstition and irrationality, even if much of the language used to talk about it is woolly and incantatory, it does not really do a great deal of harm. There is possibly some force in this. If someone believes that walking under a ladder brings bad luck, he suffers no inconvenience beyond the occasional detour of a few steps, and may even avoid drips of paint, water or cement, depending on what the man up the ladder is doing; that the belief (probably) arose originally from the connection between ladders and gallows is quite by the way. If the universities are thought to be the proud inheritors of a tradition stretching back into the Middle Ages, it may not matter that many of the traditions are (like that other ancient mediaeval survival, the Christmas tree) nineteenth-century importations from Germany, or, like the turkey, importations from America; academic illusions may contribute to the flavour of life no less than fir-trees or turkeys. Myths and superstitions even have their positive side. It has already been observed that many poets from Homer to Graves have used myths as the basis for some excellent poetry, and many others have found it a useful source of ornament at least; many scientists like Kepler have stumbled into basic discoveries while working through obsessions with theories ranging from the mystical to the downright cranky.[7] For that matter, 'traditions' of excellence and academic freedom in the universities, however dubious historically, may well have served to reinforce the sometimes very real (if recent) flourishing of these values in practice.

On the other hand, taking myths seriously can be a dangerous proceeding. In terms of efficiency, it can be a monumental distraction from thinking and acting rationally about education, at a time when there is pretty general agreement on the need for improvement, if on little else. We have already seen how shaky notions about the universities and secondary schools have clouded the issue about their relationship with other parts of the educational system; it is not easy to think sensibly about relationships on the basis of a mythical view of the things related. Reliance on myth also encourages a great deal of rationalisation (as opposed to reasoning), and reinforces some odd ideas about the nature of cause and effect, and the rules of logic and evidence. There is no need to go to the febrile columns of the *Scottish Daily Express* for examples of this – a good deal of the more temperate discussion on the curriculum, for instance, is not altogether free of the *post facto* relationship and the unsupported assertion of which we have already seen a fair amount. Worst of all, perhaps, myth may be fun but it is a shaky basis for action; we cannot all be as lucky as Kepler. Thus, it does no great harm (except in the sense that no error is harmless) to believe that the earth is a flat disc and the sun a fiery ball (or, for that matter, a flaming chariot) going round it every day. To a limited extent, one can even use this view to get *some* results – navigation, for instance, can be carried out quite adequately on a geocentric scheme of the universe (and even a flat-earth scheme will work over very short distances with a tolerable margin of error). But the extent to which a mythical view can reasonably inform action is severely limited; navigation in a geocentric universe may work on the earth's surface, but space navigation would present some quite fundamental problems. Likewise in education: myths and superstitions can be harmless enough, provided we do not intend to think too clearly about our problems or do much about them.

One of the most widely current myths which can be argued to have done most damage to the educational system and the children going through it is the one offered by the Spens Report,[8] which recommended distinct categories of schools on the assumption that children could be divided into equally distinct types, essentially the 'academic' and 'non-academic' (or, more popularly, 'bright' and 'dull' or even, in the mouths of many teachers as well as others, 'good' and 'bad').[9] The myth is much older than Spens; the classic formulation of it can be found in Plato, and has been frequently cited to this very day:

'Now I wonder if we could contrive one of these convenient stories ... some magnificent myth that would in itself carry conviction to our whole community, including, if possible, the Guardians themselves?'

'What sort of story?'

'Nothing new – a fairy story like those poets tell about the sort of thing that often happened "once upon a time", but never does now ... We shall address our citizens as follows: You are, all of you in this land, brothers. But when God fashioned you, he added gold in the composition of those of you who are qualified to be Rulers (which is why their prestige is the greatest); he put silver in the Auxiliaries, and iron and bronze in the farmers and the rest. Now since you are all of the same stock, though children will commonly resemble their parents, occasionally a silver child will be born of golden parents, or a golden child of silver parents, and so on. Therefore, the first and most important of God's commandments to the Rulers is that they must exercise their function as Guardians with particular care in watching the mixture of metals in the characters of the children. If one of their own children has bronze or iron in its make-up, they must harden their hearts, and degrade it to the ranks of the industrial and agricultural class where it properly belongs: similarly, if a child of this class is born with gold or silver in its nature, they will promote it appropriately to be a Guardian or an Auxiliary. For they know that there is a prophecy that the State will be ruined when it has Guardians of silver or bronze.'

'That is the story. Do you think there is any way of making them believe it?'

'Not in the first generation,' he said, 'but you might succeed with the second and later generations.'[10]

At least Plato realised that this was a myth, and though meaning it to be taken seriously (for propaganda purposes, as he said earlier) it was not intended to be a scientifically accurate description of clear-cut human types. But those who have accepted the Spens argument *have* made this clear division. This is not to

deny human differences, in intelligence as in other things; but
even if one *does* accept the concept of intelligence (by no means
as indisputable as many laymen think, at any rate judging from
the difficulties that psychologists have in agreeing about it);
even if one *does* accept that intelligence is unidimensional (*i.e.*
that it is a constant characteristic rather than a *set* of not always
consistent abilities), the myth of the metals and its modern variants will not stand up. The human variable of intelligence (like,
say, height) may be plotted on a continuum, with fine gradations from the least able through average to the higher ranges;
even the supporting evidence for the classical view does not
justify putting children into clearly-defined compartments, any
more than the undoubted variations in adult stature justify the
assumption that all must be five feet, five feet six inches or six
feet, with no gradations in between. (The attempts of some
clothing manufacturers to work on a system not too far removed from this have not been entirely happy.) Many educational systems, including our own, have found it convenient to
classify children into apparent categories of ability at one time
or another; but different systems at different times have drawn
the lines in different places, according largely to the availability
of room in certain types of school. The dividing lines are arbitrary, not natural; and although a case can be made for urging
that in certain practical circumstances a line has to be drawn
somewhere, this does not mean that it corresponds to any
natural division. Yet the Spens updating of Plato does just that,
and thus provides an apparent rationale for continuing apart-
heid in the educational system, making it more difficult for discussion on the best forms of secondary education to proceed
sensibly. This particular myth has contributed heavily to the
conceptual rigidity of the 'eleven-plus' and its variants (some
schools in certain cities actually operate a four-plus) which has
led primary and secondary education up a blind alley for decades – to say nothing of the personal tensions among parents,
teachers and the luckless children who have found themselves
on the wrong side of the dividing-line, and have also been led by
the myth to accept this as a blanket judgement on their ability,
intelligence and even personal worth.

As a corollary of this, feelings of superiority by some children
and inferiority by others are given an intellectual as well as a

social rationale – on the face of it a more acceptable discriminating factor in a society less prepared than it once was to support social discrimination, at least overtly. As we have already seen, both rationales are largely based on unexamined criteria, but there is more to it than this; the modern versions of the Platonic myth give to a divisive system (heavily reinforced with fake traditionalism, much of it with strong social overtones) an apparently intellectual gloss – and, in a climate which associates ability with merit (as an earlier age associated wealth with merit) even a moral gloss as well. Further, by confounding social and intellectual élitism, it can also produce considerable disorientation among 'successful' and 'deserving' working-class children. Given the grafting of a meritocratic pattern on to a school system essentially based on social class, academic success becomes a package deal – intellectually able working-class children are under almost irresistible pressure to join the middle class as the 'right' (even the only) route to success, with all kinds of personal conflicts and home–school alienations which have been amply described elsewhere, notably by Jackson and Marsden in their impressionistic but telling account.[11] The converse, however, does not so readily apply; one has to travel a long way to find the middle-class parent of an academically mediocre child who will cheerfully accept the idea that a secondary modern school and manual occupation are the 'right' place for him. Unlike Plato's Guardians, they do not 'harden their hearts', but prefer to have it both ways. It is a very human, if not very logical reaction, and there are many private schools throughout the country testifying to the reluctance of modern Guardians to carry the Platonic (or Spensian) view of the human intellect to its conclusion. The 'freedom of choice' slogan – the linch-pin of the independent and semi-independent schools – can provide a convenient escape-clause from the remorseless logic of the Platonic myth. Only up to a point, however; not only is this freedom limited to a few, as has already been argued, but it can become increasingly limited even for this group as the meritocratic justification of the divided system catches on. As the 'escape' schools are more sought after, they can afford to become more and more choosy, until the schools are selecting the children, not their parents the schools. There is a certain irony in the dilemma of parents thus having to try to reconcile a socially and intellectually élitist view of their own position; logical inconsistency is a common characteristic of myth and is liable to produce many anomalies in practice, but this is small consolation to the children themselves.

The universities have proved to be fertile ground for growing myths, and in this case at least some of them can be argued to have done little harm and even occasionally some good. But this is not always the case, for rational discussion can be pre-empted by mythical thinking as readily in universities as anywhere else. For all the appeals to the idea of a university as a place where there can be a free interplay of ideas – the republic of learning, the community of scholars – it has like any other large institution a power-structure within which people jockey for advantage. University myths help, up to a point, in making this process (sometimes) a little more bland and on occasion even a little more tolerant than would be the case in (say) a business firm or a political party; but it also does a disservice in imposing a phoney consensus ('we all share the same values at least') thus making it all too often difficult for genuine – and legitimate – differences of opinion to be discussed adequately. Further, the current myths of general academic competence (as opposed to specialist competence) go a long way towards shoring up an authoritarian power-structure. Reasonable discussion of academic matters can be bedevilled by the notion of professorial authority, widely interpreted to mean that the view of a professor of anything must carry more weight than that of anyone else, even when that someone else is a specialist in the matter under discussion and the professor is not. It is not difficult to see how this myth arose; not so long ago, the professors *were* the teaching body, and the university Senate was thus the collective of the teaching staff. But the composition of the teaching body has changed so fundamentally that the professors (heads of departments and some others) are now a definite minority; yet, in most cases, they retain the bulk of power in the higher organs of university control. Non-professorial members now have some representation – a built-in minority – and in some universities students also have a voice, though generally a small one. But the professoriate retains a special position derived from a time when there was virtually no one else; and if they have some particular characteristics that distinguish them qualitatively from the rest of their colleagues, this has yet to be demonstrated. Some of the more picturesque conflicts that can arise from this situation have become tolerably well known through the national press, but as far as we can discover practically every university in the country has some trouble-spot largely attributable to the assumption that a professor has some kind of divine right to rule and that departments are feudal fiefs. It is significant that when the 'university' (*i.e.* the Senate, or more likely the Vice-Chancellor and an inner circle, with the Senate's compliance) decides to effect some change in the work or orientation of a department, the normal method is to appoint to the relevant chair someone who they think will carry the changes through. The actual members of the department (let alone those studying in it) *may* be consulted, but it would be rash of them to expect it, or to hope that their views will carry much weight if they happen to run counter to those of the higher organs – composed, it must be stressed again, of people whose knowledge and expertise lie in other fields. The justification for this sort of thing is partly 'traditional', although the tradition is dubious in the extreme: professors in the 1970s are not, functionally, the same kind of people as they were in the 1860s. The use – and, not infrequently, the abuse – of power within the universities can no doubt be traced to simple ambition and other basic emotions and drives that can be found at work in any large organisation; but the myths that have surrounded them have at the same time strengthened them, provided them with an apparent justification, and made it more difficult for them to be recognised for what they are.

In a similar way, the corpus of myth that has grown up round the universities has made it more difficult to think dispassionately about their role. As we have seen, the claim that the universities have always concerned themselves with the pursuit of knowledge for its own sake, at a consistently high level of scholarship, is dubious to say the least, yet it is taken seriously enough to bedevil relations with those institutions of higher education more overtly and specifically concerned with vocational preparation. The ill-concealed disdain of James (already cited)[12] is a case in point, and for a more recent example one might consider the reluctance of many universities to involve themselves at all seriously in the education of teachers. The

Bachelor of Education degree, established with high hopes in the 1960s as a bridge between the universities and the colleges of education, has turned out very unevenly. In some places all appears to go relatively smoothly, while in others the universities content themselves with a rather distant and half-hearted supervision of standards, but fail to participate in the teaching to any great extent. The B.Ed. thus has some difficulty in securing acceptance as a 'real' degree at all, with the further result (following the law of self-fulfilling prophecies) that it all too frequently *becomes* a second-class qualification, thus confirming the original assumption, widespread in the universities, that the training of teachers (unlike the training of doctors, dentists, lawyers, vets and ministers, and even businessmen) is not academically respectable. There are strong indications that this stems not from any real disdain for vocational studies as such (as we have seen from the ready acceptance now accorded to the more prestigious vocational studies such as medicine or law) but rather from the social prestige (or lack of it) with which these studies are associated. Nursing, librarianship or teaching are no more vocational than dentistry or law, but nurses and teachers are notably less well paid. The reluctance of certain English universities to accept medicine as academically respectable until the social and financial position of doctors improved provides an instructive parallel. Nor is it easy to take very seriously the objection that certain disciplines are intrinsically unworthy; such judgements are, after all, made by academics whose knowledge of the proposed new fields of study is bound to be slight, and whose machinery for judging it is, to say the least, unsophisticated. We know of one university where a committee investigating the continued acceptability of a course consisted *entirely* of people from other (and often remote) disciplines, and solemnly set themselves to judge the merits of the subject from course-outlines (with due attention to the length of reading-lists) and the quality of the teaching from past students' examination scripts; at the same time they ignored the views of external examiners and assessors, who *were* specialists in the field. Their findings were unfavourable, but were overturned by the university Senate, which happened to contain enough people with a certain scepticism about the validity of the judgement; but it was a near thing, and others have been less lucky.

Ironically, where resistance to 'new' disciplines, especially vocational ones, has broken down, this has been in areas where large sums of money are involved rather than from any re-examination of the 'academic respectability' argument. In one Scottish university, the contrast between the long struggles to gain acceptance for a chair of nursing studies, and the establishment of a chair of fire engineering (externally financed) virtually on the nod, has not passed unnoticed. There have been many examples of this kind of thing in the last few years; and yet the notion that some studies are intrinsically worthy of inclusion in the university syllabus, while others (mainly vocational) are not, persists. The power of myth to influence policy is clear enough here. The same goes, by the way, for 'university standards', generally thought of as something immutable, innate, absolute and instantly recognisable by academics. There has been some controversy of late whether university standards are rising or falling; by most objective criteria (such as the level of entrance requirements) the general consensus among specialists is that there has been a steady rise since the war, though some, using rather different and more impressionistic criteria, have questioned this. What should be clear is that they are at least not immutable; and as our historical enquiry has shown, it is not all that long since the universities – or any other kind of educational institution, for that matter – had no particular notion of distinctive academic standards at all, as witness the long-standing ambiguity of the roles of universities, colleges and secondary schools. Where there is a will to believe, however, a way will be found, and awkward evidence is liable to be pushed to one side. It is striking how rarely the universities are prepared to use the techniques, of disinterested searching enquiry, often claimed as peculiarly their own, on themselves.

Most seriously of all, perhaps, myth in general serves to rationalise self-interest. This is true even when the myths are believed by the mythologisers themselves – all the more true, perhaps, since they are not necessarily any more dishonest or self-seeking than anyone else, and the belief that their motives are simon-pure can put added sinew into their resolve to defend their interests. Few people are as resolute in holding what they have than those who can convince themselves that it is also for the 'general good', or the gods, or freedom, or the maintenance of standards, or whatever. There is no particular reason to think that the priests who did very nicely out of temple offerings and sacrifices did not also believe that these were equally pleasing to the gods (to whom they burned thighbones wrapped in fat while they ate the meat on the gods' behalf). Now, this position, as we have suggested already, is not self-evidently ridiculous. It *could* be argued that whatever privileges independent and grammar schools confer on a minority, a specially-treated élite is necessary to the well-being of society as a whole; it could be that the universities, whatever their real role in the past, now do have a special position as centres of excellence, pace-makers, patrons of research and guardians of intellectual freedom; it could be the case that out of the welter of interested parties concerned with the control of a school, the headmaster occupies such a special position as to justify substantial independence from immediate local authority supervision and near-dictatorial powers over his staff and pupils, which he will have the sense not to abuse; it could be that men appointed to run individual university departments because of their specialist expertise have accumulated such a store of generalised wisdom that they are fit to pronounce finally upon anything else; it could even be the case that particular types of formal instruction prepare people better than any other way to run a university, a college, a school or a classroom. All of these decisions involve conferring upon certain people some considerable benefits in terms of power, prestige, payment, or any combination of these, but if this works or makes sense on other grounds then there could be a case for regarding this as a necessary part of the deal. But there are rather few attempts to argue like this. Nor, to be fair, are arguments from naked self-interest all that common (though the current controversies over selective schooling do provide some);[13] self-interest is a powerful motive, but a weak argument when directed at those whose interest is not involved. Instead, therefore, we get the myths, the superstitions, the incantations – 'freedom of choice' or 'variety' or 'long tradition of excellence' to justify privilege in schooling; the conjuring up of spurious traditions, rather than an examination of present functions, to defend the universities' special place in the educational system; 'independence of the school' to buttress the powerful position of many headmasters *vis-à-vis* their own colleagues and pupils (this holds good for the heads of not a few colleges too); 'academic judgement' (culled from a time when the area of learning was vastly smaller than it is now) to shore up professorial privilege; and a host of appeals to tradition (again) to preserve the position of subjects, courses or the institutions offering them, instead of recognising their importance to those who offer them or those who have acquired the qualifications and naturally wish to keep up the value of their currency.

For some, then, we do not need to look very far to explain the power which educational myth exerts; it is far too valuable to let go. But this cannot be the whole story, for it would not work if only the beneficiaries believed it; in terms of sheer numbers, most of the deference – to say nothing of the money – has to come from the worshippers rather than the priests and deacons, from those at the wrong end of the distancing mechanisms. Some, possibly, have simply been bemused into a vague sense of awe; for some, too, like the family of Brecht's little monk,[14] some kind of order even when based on delusion seems preferable to no order at all. It is not surprising, perhaps, that the relatively unsophisticated parent of a child who has failed the eleven-plus accepts the psychologically dubious techniques as the verdict of science; more generally, at a time of accelerating change, the claim that institutions or courses or subjects have 'stood the test of time' has a fairly wide appeal, especially if it is not realised that time has done its testing for a shorter period than is usually claimed. It would seem that the very existence of continuity (however tenuous in fact) strikes a responsive chord in a great many people, unable or disinclined to take a more critical look at the claims and their implications. Deference also has its devotees; in some cases this may be little more than forelock-tugging, but perhaps more generally it offers the comfort of knowing what is what without having to think or worry too much about it. One suburban mother recently defended selective schools by saying, 'Oh, but the teachers there all have degrees and diplomas and things', and was not pleased to be told that this was true (by law) of every other school in the city; a fixed point in the universe had become unfixed and she felt uncomfortable. With teachers, as with doctors, dentists, lawyers and all the rest, it is not only the practitioners that gain comfort from the myths that enhance their position; so do their customers – few people under medical care wish to be made too aware of how far their physicians are from omniscience, for the sake of their peace of mind. The same holds good for those under the care of the educational system which, in the roles of pupil and parent, includes practically everybody at one time or another. If the stripping away of myth reveals shaky foundations, there might be an obligation to do something about it, or at least to think clearly about it, which is not a comfortable experience. Perhaps it is true that, as Shaw put it, 'Liberty means responsibility; that is why most men dread it.'[15]

For some others, who perhaps ought to know better, the reverse process serves to perpetuate educational myth. Everyone has been to school, therefore everyone knows all about education. (Not quite everything, perhaps – they may concede ignorance on some technical points, and leave these to 'experts' – ironically, these are frequently matters, like testing, where the experts are either at loggerheads or are very careful not to make exaggerated claims for their techniques.) But at least they are confident of their capacity to pronounce on fundamentals. This may take the form of assuming that things as they are (or, more commonly, as they were) are more or less all right or, alternatively, that educational ideas and procedures can be made subject to the same kind of judgement as one applies to styles of dress. It frequently takes the form of disdain for education as a subject, a feeling that it is hardly the sort of thing one *studies* (a common view among academics and school-teachers alike, but owing more to *social* disdain on the one hand and the practitioner's resentment of the back-room boys on the other than to any close analysis). In this case, accepting myths is much less trouble – it has the combined attractions of reinforcing self-esteem, providing an apparent security for one's intellectual position, and requiring the minimum of intellectual effort and no painful reappraisal of basic ideas. This is a formidable combination, and one which brings comfort to many, practitioner and lay alike. The trouble is that so much of it is founded on delusion, which is not the best basis for thought; and, against the crumbs of comfort many find in the myths, we must set the bunglings, the snobberies, the neuroses, the institutional scleroses and the not inconsiderable contributions to the sum of human unhappiness that can be traced to taking myths at face-value. One possible view of education (to which the authors subscribe) is that education should be among other things a liberating experience for teacher and taught alike. All too often it is far from that, and it will take a great deal of thought and effort to make it a reality (if this is what we really want, rather than yet another pious slogan). If education is to liberate, it must itself be liberated; this will take some doing, and will involve much fundamental – and legitimate – disagreement on what this should mean and how it should be achieved, but one essential step is to be continually prepared to identify and clear away the web of myth which from time to time constrains it.

REFERENCES

1. Knox's *First Book of Discipline* (1560) was certainly an early example of a scheme for a national system of education from primary school to university, with provision for compulsory attendance, promotion to higher stages by talent, student maintenance grants, etc. But a scheme it remained: the Scottish Parliament turned it down, and although some of the provisions did come into effect later, and although Scotland (along with Prussia, the Netherlands, and certain Swiss cantons and New England colonies) had developed a national system of sorts by the eighteenth century, the all-embracing open system of the kind envisaged by Knox had to wait, as elsewhere, until relatively modern times.

2. Robert Graves, *The Greek Myths* (Penguin, 1954), Vol. 1, p. 10.

3. The idea has been around rather longer; it was much bandied about, for example, in a Commons debate on comprehensive education in January 1965.

4. At a 'Freedom of Choice' rally (in favour of selective schools) in Glasgow on 23 March 1972.

5. Charles Graham, 'Whacko, Mr Campbell', *Scottish Daily Express*, Friday, 24 March 1972. (As a further exercise in sophisticated educational argument, the article is accompanied by a Cummings cartoon depicting the headmaster's study in 'comprehensive school – 1800 pupils'; the head is indicating an enormous lout to a pair of rather baffled parents, and declaring: 'Raising the school leaving age has been a great success. Though your little Percy can't read or write, we've managed to get him through his 'O' levels in Vandalism, Violence and Pot-Smoking.')

6. 'The central folly and absurdity which cries aloud to be denounced is student participation. There is no, repeat no, rational justification for students to participate in the academic or admini-

strative or disciplinary management of the universities. The whole idea is utterly nonsensical.' Rt. Hon, J. Enoch Powell, MP, speech to the Northern Universities Dinner of the Federation of Conservative Students at the Chase Hotel, York, Saturday, 7 March 1970.

7. See p. 8.

8. *Report of the Consultative Committee on Secondary Education* (*The Spens Report*), H.M.S.O., 1938.

9. There are striking variations in the numbers thought suitable for each group from one system to another, or even within one system; consider, for example, the discrepancies in the proportion going to grammar school in different parts of England.

10. Plato, *The Republic*, III (Penguin edition, Pt. IV, pp. 160–1, 1955).

11. Brian Jackson and Dennis Marsden, *Education and the Working Class* (Penguin, 1966).

12. See pp. 47–48.

13. Economists' objections to the introduction of a sociology Tripos in Cambridge were, however, more than usually frank; they foresaw redundancy among economists as a result.

14. B. Brecht, *Leben des Galilei*, 8 (Suhrkamp Verlag, 1970), pp. 75–6.

15. Bernard Shaw, *The Revolutionists' Handbook* (app. to *Man and Superman*).

INDEX

Other Panthers For Your Enjoyment

More Non-Fiction